ROUTLEDGE LIBRARY EDITIONS:
LANDMARKS IN THE HISTORY OF
ECONOMIC THOUGHT

Volume 5

T0341280

THE NATURAL SYSTEM OF
POLITICAL ECONOMY

THE NATURAL SYSTEM OF POLITICAL ECONOMY

1837

FRIEDRICH LIST
Translated and edited by
W. O. Henderson

Routledge
Taylor & Francis Group

LONDON AND NEW YORK

First published in 1983 by Frank Cass and Company Limited

This edition first published in 2017
by Routledge
2 Park Square, Milton Park, Abingdon, Oxon OX14 4RN

and by Routledge
711 Third Avenue, New York, NY 10017

Routledge is an imprint of the Taylor & Francis Group, an informa business

British Library Cataloguing in Publication Data
A catalogue record for this book is available from the British Library

ISBN: 978-1-138-21086-8 (Set)
ISBN: 978-1-315-40933-7 (Set) (ebk)
ISBN: 978-1-138-21646-4 (Volume 5) (hbk)
ISBN: 978-1-138-21650-1 (Volume 5) (pbk)
ISBN: 978-1-315-44224-2 (Volume 5) (ebk)

Publisher's Note
The publisher has gone to great lengths to ensure the quality of this reprint but points out that some imperfections in the original copies may be apparent.

Disclaimer
The publisher has made every effort to trace copyright holders and would welcome correspondence from those they have been unable to trace.

FRIEDRICH LIST

THE NATURAL SYSTEM
OF POLITICAL ECONOMY
1837

Translated and edited by
W. O. HENDERSON

FRANK CASS

First published 1983 in Great Britain by
FRANK CASS AND COMPANY LIMITED
Gainsborough House, 11 Gainsborough Road,
London E11 1RS, England

and in the United States of America by
FRANK CASS AND COMPANY LIMITED
c/o Biblio Distribution Centre
81 Adams Drive, P.O. Box 327, Totowa, N.J. 07511

British Library Cataloguing in Publication Data

List, Friedrich
    The natural system of political economy 1837.
    1. Microeconomics
    I. Title   II. Henderson, W.O.   III. Das nationale
    System der politischen Oekonomie. *English*
    338.5   HB171.5

ISBN 0-7146-3206-6

Typeset by John Smith, London
Printed in Great Britain by
T. J. Press (Padstow) Ltd.,
Padstow, Cornwall

CONTENTS

CONTENTS

EDITOR'S INTRODUCTION

FRIEDRICH LIST, a leading German economist and journalist in the first half of the nineteenth century, was one of the earliest and severest critics of the classical school of economists. He denounced Adam Smith and his disciples as the "cosmopolitan school" and advocated what he called first a "natural" and then a "national" doctrine of economics. He held that universal free trade was an ideal that might be achieved in the far distant future but, for the time being, each nation should foster the development of its own manufactures by prohibitions, import duties, subsidies, and navigation laws so as to restrict the flow of imports from more advanced industrial countries. Only by such means could countries like France, Germany, Russia, and the United States ever hope to reach a standard of industrial efficiency which would enable them to compete on equal terms with Britain which was at that time by far the most advanced manufacturing country in the world.

List was no mere armchair critic of the free traders. He had taken an active part in fiscal controversies in America and in Germany. In the United States, where he lived from 1825 to 1832 (except for an interval of a year),[1] List had become involved in the struggle between protectionists and free traders that preceded the passing of a new tariff law in 1828. He had vigorously supported the propaganda campaign in favour of higher import duties mounted by the Philadelphia Society for the Promotion of Manufactures and the Mechanic Arts. In a series of letters to Charles Ingersoll, published in the *National Gazette* (Philadelphia) in 1827, List had argued in favour of greater protection for the American iron and textile industries. In the same year the letters appeared in two pamphlets entitled *Outlines of American Political Economy* and *Appendix to the Outlines of American Political Economy.*[2]

In Germany List had taken a leading part in the agitation in favour of protection. In 1819, as a young man, he had drawn up a

1

petition on behalf of a Union of German Merchants for submission to the Federal Diet in which he had urged the German states to set up a customs union with a tariff "based upon the principle of retaliation against foreign countries". For eighteen months he had been an indefatigable supporter of the Union of Merchants and had worked hard to promote its objects.[3] Later, in the 1840s, in the early years of the German customs union (*Zollverein*) List argued that German manufacturers were at the mercy of competition from highly efficient English rivals and urgently needed greater tariff protection in the home market. In his view a great mistake had been made in 1834 when the states joining the Zollverein had agreed to adopt the Prussian tariff in 1818 which at that time was the most liberal in Europe.

List's book on *The National System of Political Economy: International Commerce, Commercial Policy, and the German Customs Union*, published in 1841,[4] came to be accepted as a standard statement of the protectionist case. Long after List's death advocates of protection found in List's writings the arguments they were seeking to justify their demands for higher tariffs. In 1889, three years before his appointment as Russia's Minister of Finance, Count Witte wrote that List's book was studied in every German university and lay on Bismarck's desk.[5] In 1909 F. W. Hirst declared that "it is not too much to say that most of the ideas which underlie modern tariffs, both in the old world and the new, were originated and formulated by List".[6]

List's disciples, however, treated the doctrines of their master in a rather cavalier fashion. They paid tribute to the profundity of List's learning and the cogency of his arguments but instead of following his advice in its entirety they accepted those aspects of his theories that suited their immediate purpose and ignored those that did not. For example List had demanded protection only for manufactured goods and had recommended that no import duties should be levied upon agricultural products or raw materials. In practice, however, whenever a country has adopted the policy of protection the landowners and farmers have declared that if manufacturers enjoy a privileged position in the home market they too have a right to receive similar privileges. And although taxes on food normally result in higher prices for the housewife, few governments have been able to resist demands for protection from the agricultural interest. Moreover very few protectionists were prepared to face the possibility – clearly envisaged by List – that manufacturers should at some time in the future be prepared to dispense with the protection afforded by import duties or subsidies. List advocated protection mainly for new "infant" industries during the first years of their development to give them an opportunity to become as efficient as similar industries already established in more advanced countries. He recognised that, at any rate for a time, this would involve some sacrifice on the part of consumers who would have to pay high prices for goods of comparatively poor quality instead of buying better products from abroad more cheaply. But however long an "infant" industry enjoys protection it is rare indeed for manufacturers to admit that their industry has grown up and no longer requires protection. Those who impose tariffs on "infant" industries may intend that the duties should be levied only for a time and should be lowered or even abolished when the industry has become well established. In practice "infant" industries never seem to grow up and the duties levied to protect them become a permanent feature of the tariff. This was by no means what List had intended. Again List believed in the possibility of universal free trade in the future. His disciples rarely shared his optimism.

In addition to the *Outlines of American Political Economy* and *The National System of Political Economy* List had a third book to his credit but this was not published until ninety years after it had been written.[7] This was *The Natural System of Political Economy* which was written in Paris in the autumn of 1837. When List arrived in France at the end of October he apparently had no intention of resuming his studies on economics. During the previous four years he had tried to foster the progress of railway construction in Germany and he had been particularly active in promoting the line between Leipzig and Dresden. Disappointed at his failure to secure either a directorship in a railway company or a post in the administration of a state railway, he had left Germany to settle in Paris, where he hoped to arouse interest in his plans for the construction of railways in France.

Soon after his arrival in Paris, where he found lodgings in the Rue des Martyrs, List learned that the Academy of Moral and Political Sciences[8] was offering a prize for a treatise answering the question: "If a country proposes to introduce free trade or to modify its tariff, what factors should it take into account so as to reconcile in the fairest manner the interests of producers with those of consumers?"

3

Although the closing date for entries was December 31, 1837 List decided to compete for the prize and the manuscript was completed in great haste. On November 22 List wrote to his wife that he was working for fifteen hours a day to finish the treatise in time.[9] When he submitted his manuscript he was told that the final date for submitting it had been postponed for a week, so he was able to make some last minute revisions. On the day on which the final corrections were made List added a long note to Chapter 4 in which he stated that the manuscript had taken forty days to complete and in a letter to his wife he declared that he had spent six or seven weeks on the treatise.[10] Later he pretended that the work had been done more quickly than this. In 1838 he wrote that his manuscript had been finished in three weeks[11] and in 1841 he asserted that he "had only a fortnight ... to meet the Academy's peremptory deadline". List was also mistaken in 1841 when he wrote that "as I did not have my earlier writings by me, I had to rely entirely on my memory".[12] In fact List had consulted over thirty books.[13] An examination of the manuscript shows that these books included standard works of leading writers on trade and industry – King, Anderson, and Adam Smith on England; Chaptal, Dupin, Say, and Ferrier on France; Uztaris and Ulloa on Spain; Alexander Hamilton and Mathew Carey on the United States; and Storch on Russia.

In writing his thesis List was influenced by the advice given to competitors on behalf of the Academy by the well known economist Charles Dupin. The "Programme" drawn up by Dupin raised a number of questions which competitors were expected to answer. Was it right that cheap foreign imports should be allowed to ruin a branch of industry at home in the name of Free Trade? Should industries that had developed during a war (to produce goods in short supply) be allowed to sink into oblivion when hostilities ceased? Would it be in the national interest to protect an industry which could not compete with a foreign rival because that rival had gained an advantage by using a newly invented efficient machine? And should the state foster the growth of a new industry by a protective tariff and by encouraging skilled foreign mechanics to settle in France? In his essay List attempted to answer these – and other – questions posed by Dupin.

The Academy decided that none of the twenty seven manuscripts submitted was worthy of the prize. It criticised the candidates for failing to answer the question that had been set. They had been content to advocate either a policy of complete freedom of trade or one of protection. Three manuscripts, however, were commended as "ouvrages remarquables" and one of them bore the motto "Et la patrie et l'humanité". This was List's treatise. List was bitterly disappointed at not receiving the prize. He needed the money and he would have welcomed the prestige attached to an award from the leading learned institute in Europe. And the publication of a prize essay would have established List's reputation as an economist. List was angry that the adjudicators had failed to appreciate the merits of *The Natural System of Political Economy*. In a letter to Cotta he complained that the Academy had not merely failed to award him the prize but had added insult to injury by announcing a new competition with the German customs union as its subject. List declared that he had already dealt fully with the significance of the Zollverein in his manuscript and he quoted with approval a remark made to him by "an influential personage" in Paris that the Academy was "a nest of robbers".[14]

Having failed to win the prize, List dismissed *The Natural System of Political Economy* as a hastily written work of no great importance and turned his attention to *The National System of Political Economy* which appeared in 1841. Although the manuscript submitted in the competition gathered dust in the archives of the French Academy until its publication in 1927 it is much more than a mere first draft of *The National System of Political Economy*. It is a book in its own right which marks an important stage in the progress of List's economic thinking. Since List had to meet a deadline he had to be brief and he had to put forward his arguments in a concise form. Although the treatise was only about half the length of *The National System of Political Economy* it contains virtually all the main points to be found in the later work. As the editors of *The Natural System of Political Economy* observe:

> List's more important and fundamental teachings are fully developed in this book. Above all the theory of the stages of economic growth finds full classic expression as a central theme in List's thinking – as it does again in *The National System of Political Economy*. In his treatise List frequently gives clear, systematic, and brief explanations in numbered paragraphs of his most important doctrines, which are not so clearly stated in any of his other works.[15]

The importance of *The Natural System of Political Economy* lies not so much in List's advocacy of the policy of protection as in the new – or relatively new – doctrines that he put forward. While the classical economists had examined problems concerning population, exchange-value, money, rent, and the allocation of scarce resources, List discussed stages of economic growth, "productive power," and the industrialisation of backward regions. Those who have regarded List simply as a leading protectionist have done him less than justice and have failed to appreciate the real significance of his writings. There was no lack of champions of the policy of protection in the early nineteenth century. Chaptal, Dupin, and Ferrier in France, and Alexander Hamilton and Mathew Carey in the United States had advocated the imposition of prohibitions and of import duties to safeguard native industries, while in England there was ample support for the Corn Laws, the navigation code, and imperial preference. But List offered his readers much more than a repetition of the familiar arguments put forward by these writers. He regarded prohibitions, import duties, and subsidies as simply one method – indeed the most important method – by which a government could foster a nation's economic expansion. But in his view a tariff was only a means to an end. And the object of the policy of protection, from List's point of view, was the establishment of an urban-industrial society. This was the promised land to which List believed that he could lead those who accepted his doctrines and followed the policies that he recommended.

List declared that in a purely agrarian and rural society "the whole range of intellectual and moral powers is virtually non-existent" and sheer physical strength was all that could be expected from those who worked on the land. On the other hand an industrialised urban society "calls forth and promotes the growth of intellectual and moral forces of every kind". List considered that "industry is the mother and father of science, literature, the arts, enlightenment, freedom, useful institutions, and national power and independence".[16] He regarded a manufacturing town as a mecca for enterprising entrepreneurs and skilled workers who could fulfil their ambitions in a way that would be impossible in the countryside. He saw in the growth of factory towns the key to educational and cultural advance. Only an urban and industrial society could afford to provide its citizens with facilities for progress in the arts and sciences. Only such a civilisation could build and maintain schools, colleges, theatres, opera houses, concert halls, museums, and art galleries. But what List failed to mention was that the factory workers of the 1830s had to work long hours for low wages. Many of them lived in wretched slums, survived on a very poor diet, and suffered from numerous industrial diseases. They had no security of employment and ran a serious risk of losing their jobs whenever there was a slump in trade. For them there was no hope of the good life in factory towns that List had promised them. The idyllic existence of the urban workers was a figment of List's lively imagination and bore no resemblance to the harsh reality of life in a factory town at that time.

List next explained how a backward country could foster the growth of its economy so that it could eventually enjoy the benefits of an urban industrial society. He believed that this could be done by fostering a country's "productive powers". These were rather different from the "productive forces" discussed by Charles Dupin in a statistical work on the French economy published in 1827.[17] Dupin had explained that "by productive and commercial forces in France I mean the combined forces exercised by men, animals and nature and applied to work in agriculture, workshops, and commercial enterprises". List's doctrine of "productive powers" was much wider than this for it included political, administrative, and social institutions, natural and human resources, industrial establishments, and public works.

List held that before a country could foster the growth of its "productive powers" it should have made some progress towards the establishment of suitable political and social institutions. The abolition of slavery and serfdom, the ending of despotism and autocracy, the establishment of the rule of law with security for persons and property were essential prerequisites for economic growth. A measure of self-government at both local and national level was also highly desirable. The natural resources of a country, particularly its land and minerals, should be used to the best advantage. If coal, peat, timber, or iron ore were available they could become the basis of important industries. The skills of the people – especially the young people – should be fostered by providing a sound elementary education for all children and adequate training facilities at universities and technical colleges for the more gifted. A well educated community, with a sufficient number of competent managers and skilled workers, could exploit a country's

7

natural resources far more efficiently than a backward ignorant people. List included professional men, civil servants, and local government officials among those who helped to increase a nation's "productive powers". While this section of the community did not grow foodstuffs or make manufactured goods it did assist indirectly in their production. The lawyers and policemen who maintained law and order, the armed forces which defended the country, the doctors who maintained a nation's health, the teachers who educated the rising generation, and the clergy who maintained the moral standards of their parishioners were all just as useful members of society as miners or factory workers.

The building of new factories and the opening up of new mines would not only stimulate industrial output at once but would be an asset to future generations for years to come. List considered the provision, whether by public authorities or private companies, of improved transport facilities to be a vitally important contribution to a country's "productive powers". The construction of an adequate network of roads, railways, and canals and the building of bridges and harbours were essential to promote the flow of raw materials to factories and of manufactured goods to consumers at home and abroad. List wrote with some authority on transport since he had been closely involved with the construction of the Tamaqua—Port Clinton railway in Pennsylvania and the Leipzig—Dresden railway in Saxony. The growth of the mercantile marine and the shipbuilding and fishing industries would promote the expansion of foreign trade. List also suggested other means of stimulating a nation's "productive powers" such as organising industrial exhibitions, rewarding inventors, encouraging the immigration of skilled workers from abroad, and assisting manufacturers to visit foreign factories.

List considered that none of these methods of promoting the development of a nation's "productive powers" was as effective as the imposition of prohibitions and import duties so as to protect manufacturers from competition in the home market from more advanced industrial countries. He advocated protection for new industries that could not otherwise survive competition from more efficient foreign rivals. On the other hand he considered that no protection was necessary for agriculture. The degree of protection for industry that List proposed would vary from country to country and from commodity to commodity. Some manufacturers might need to be safeguarded by prohibiting all imports of foreign goods, while others would need only the protection of moderate import duties. List believed that duties should be changed quickly if necessary. For example the sudden arrival of large quantities of a particular product should be countered at once by raising the import duty that they had to pay. List was well aware of the drawbacks of tariffs. Prohibitions and high import duties raised the prices that consumers had to pay, rendered householders liable to have their premises searched for contraband, and encouraged smuggling. But circumstances might arise which would make it imperative for a government to impose a general tariff. For example, large quantities of British manufactured goods had been sent to the Continent immediately after the collapse of the Continental System so that industries which had developed during the Napoleonic wars were threatened with extinction. Only the erection of tariff barriers enabled them to survive.

The various ways in which List suggested that a country's "productive powers" might be fostered involved sacrifices on the part of the public. The imposition of prohibitions or import duties would mean that, at any rate for a time, people would have to buy expensive goods of poor quality instead of cheap foreign goods of high quality. People would have to pay higher taxes to finance the construction of roads and canals, the establishment of technical colleges, and the holding of industrial exhibitions. List considered that it was not unreasonable to expect people to make financial sacrifices of this kind to promote the future economic prosperity of the country. As private citizens they made sacrifices for their children and grandchildren. A landowner who gave his son a good education and let him travel abroad to improve his knowledge of agricultural practices was spending money to ensure that his estate would be well run when he retired. A farmer who planted an orchard might derive little benefit from it himself but his descendants would be grateful to him for his foresight. List believed that what prudent private citizens did for later generations should also be done by the state and he urged that immediate gains should be sacrificed to ensure the economic growth of the nation in the future.

List also put forward a theory of stages of economic growth. The criterion which he used to identify different phases of growth was the extent to which the economy of a village, a region, or a nation was linked with other economies. List's first stage of economic development was one of isolation and self-sufficiency when peasants and craftsmen produced the food and manufactured goods that they required and when a village had very little contact with neighbouring communites. The second stage came when villages had made contact with the nearest town. This association with an urban economy brought new ideas and techniques to peasants and artisans. There was progress in farming and craft work and there was an exchange of commodities between urban and rural areas.

List's third phase was one in which – with improved communications – urban and rural workshops and factories were able to supply a whole country with manufactured goods. Just as an isolated village had been virtually self-sufficient in the first phase of economic development, so now in the third phase an entire country was virtually self-sufficient. In the fourth phase a nation had made contact with neighbouring states and imported some of the raw materials and foodstuffs which it required and it exported some of its manufactured goods in return. All this may appear somewhat elementary in comparison with more sophisticated modern theories of economic expansion but List deserves credit for having suggested the possibility of identifying phases of economic growth.

The merit of List's *The Natural System of Political Economy* lay in its new approach to economics, the analysis of national "productive powers," and the theory of stages of economic growth. It dealt with problems that continued to be relevant long after List's death. In the second half of the twentieth century those interested in stimulating the economic expansion of states in the Third World could still find inspiration in List's doctrines. List's true claim to fame was as "a prophet of the ambitions of all underdeveloped countries"[18] rather than as a champion of the policy of protection.

But *The Natural System of Political Economy* was not without its faults. List persistently overrated the extent to which the government of a country is capable of stimulating economic expansion. Time and time again he attributed the prosperity of a nation at a particular time to the wise actions of the government. The growth of industry and trade is a highly complex process involving the interaction of many factors. Government policy is one of these factors and it is not necessarily the most important. List's interpretation of historical events was not always accurate. He repeatedly argued that the Continental System had brought prosperity to Napoleon's dominions and that the opening of the ports after his defeat was followed by a period of depression because the markets of the Continent were flooded by cheap British manufactured goods. It is a travesty of the truth to suggest that the economies of France and her satellites flourished in Napoleon's day. Some regions – such as Saxony and the Roer Department – and some branches of manufacture derived benefits from the Emperor's economic policy. Others did not. The Grand Duchy of Berg, which included the Ruhr, "suffered nothing but injury from the Continental System".[19] And Heckscher considers that between 1811 and 1813 there was "a serious deterioration of the economic conditions prevailing everywhere on the Napoleonic mainland".[20] Again, List stated that interest rates were always high in the early stages of industrialisation. This was true of France at the time when List was writing but it had not been true of England in the second half of the eighteenth century.[21]

List was prone to make confident assertions without attempting to prove that they were correct. An example of this was his extraordinary statement that no suitable work was available for women, children, and old people on the land. Another example was his statements concerning the relationship between a country's internal and external commerce which are of no great value in the absence – at that time – of statistics of internal trade. Another weakness of List's writing was his habit of regarding "industrialists" and "agriculturalists" as compact social groups each pursuing its own economic interests. But manufacturers do not all think alike and those who make a living on the land do not all think alike. Different industrialists (ironmasters, textile manufacturers) and different "agriculturalists" (sheep farmers, dairy farmers, arable farmers, stockbreeders) may have conflicting interests and may support different fiscal policies at various times. And within a particular industry there may be groups which have different interests such as spinners, weavers, bleachers, and dyers in the textile industries.

On a number of matters on which his readers might expect some precise information List is somewhat vague. A protective tariff was the very cornerstone of his doctrine of the growth of "productive powers" which would promote industrialisation. Yet List refers only to "reasonable" and "fair" tariffs without explaining what rates of import duty are "reasonable" and "fair". The same criticism may be made concerning his reference to a "fair" rate of

11

interest, without any explanation being given as to what a "fair" rate might be.

A comment should also be made upon List's violent attack upon merchants, which is a little surprising as at one time he played a leading part in organising a Union of Merchants in Germany. List denounced merchants for what he regarded as their anti-social activities. He accused them of selling anything to anybody – so long as they had bought in the cheapest market and were selling in the dearest market – without being concerned about the way in which their transactions might affect the interests of the country. He denounced trafficking in arms and drugs. He seemed to forget that there were individuals engaged in many other occupations who were also from time to time guilty of unsocial or unpatriotic acts. There seems to be no reason to signal out the black sheep among the merchants for special condemnation.

Finally, List's criticism of Adam Smith and his followers deserves to be mentioned. List labelled Adam Smith's doctrines "cosmopolitan economics" and declared that they were based upon the principle of universal peace. List considered that "cosmopolitan economics" taught that "conflicts between nations – whether settled by force of arms or by other means – must be replaced by an alliance of all peoples, governed by laws of universal application. A world republic, as envisaged by J. B. Say, is necessary to secure the fulfilment of the dreams of the free traders".[22] List was wrong in supposing that Adam Smith chose to ignore the fact that the world was divided into many nations each of which pursued its own economic and political interests. Adam Smith had made it clear that the first duty of a sovereign was to protect a country from invasion by another state and this duty could be performed only by maintaining a military force. He declared that the art of war was the noblest of the arts. He approved of bounties on the export of sailcloth and gunpowder to encourage the production of commodities which would be of vital importance to a country in time of war. And in an oft-quoted passage he declared that since defence "is of much more importance than opulence, the act of navigation is, perhaps, the wisest of all the commercial regulations of England".[23] It may be added that List "made the mistake so common with popular writers, but inexcusable in the author of a systematic treatise, of attributing to Adam Smith the extravagant dogmas of his exponents".[24]

Some of the weaknesses of *The Natural System of Political*

12

Economy may be ascribed to List's background and previous experience. Although for a short time he had once been a professor at the University of Tübingen, he was no academic. He was a politician, a journalist, and a businessman. His treatise for the French Academy was his first attempt to give a full account of his economic doctrines. And it did not turn out to be a balanced scholarly monograph. Each chapter might have been an article written for a newspaper. It was List the journalist, rather than List the economist who was responsible for the sweeping generalisations, the exaggerations, and the personal attacks upon his opponents.

NOTES

1. List lived in the United States from June 1825 to July 1832. He was in Europe between November 1830 and October 1831.
2. Reprinted in Margaret E. Hirst, *Life of Friedrich List* (1909), pp. 147-272 and F. List, *Werke*, Vol. II (ed. W. Notz, 1931 and 1971), pp. 97-155. List's letter of November 27, 1827 was not included either in the *Outlines of American Political Economy* (1827) or in Hirst's biography of List. It is printed in F. List, *Werke*, Vol. II, pp. 155-6.
3. Hans-Peter Olshausen, *Friedrich List und der Deutsche Handels- und Gewerbsverein* (1935).
4. There are two English translations. The first (by G.A. Matile) appeared in Philadelphia in 1856, the second (by Sampson S. Lloyd) in London in 1885 (reprinted in 1904 and in 1966). A French translation by Henri Richelot was published in 1857 and a Russian translation in 1891.
5. Theodore H. Von Laue, *Sergei Witte and the Industrialisation of Russia* (1963). p. 62.
6. F.W. Hirst's introduction to Margaret E. Hirst, *Life of Friedrich List* (1909).
7. On March 15, 1913 Eugène d'Eichthal gave a lecture to the Academy of Moral and Political Sciences on the manuscript of *The Natural System of Political Economy* entitled "L'Economiste Frédéric List. Candidat à un des concours de l'Académie des sciences morales et politiques en 1837". List's manuscript was published in 1927 (reprinted 1971) as the fourth volume of his collected works. A German translation appeared in the same volume.
8. The French Academy of Moral and Political Sciences was established in 1795 as the second section of the Institute of Sciences and Arts. The section was abolished in 1802 but was revived in 1832.
9. F. List to Caroline List, November 22, 1837 in F. List, *Werke*, Vol. IV, p. 46. In this letter List stated that he was working on *two* prize essays. The second was an answer to the question: "How do the mechanical power and the means of transport now in use influence the life of the community, the state of society, the political power, and the economic development of the old world and the new?". No copy of this thesis has been found in the archives of the French Institute. Carl

Brinkmann doubts if it was ever written: see Carl Brinkmann, *Friedrich List* (1949), p. 233, note 11.
10. F. List to Caroline List, January 1, 1838 and postscript of January 13, 1838 in F. List, *Werke*, Vol. IV, pp. 47-8.
11. F. List to J.G. Cotta, September 6, 1838 in F. List, *Werke*, Vol. IV, p. 48.
12. F. List, *Das Nationale System der Politischen Ökonomie* in F. List, *Werke*, Vol. VI, p. 19.
13. F. List to Caroline List, January 1, 1838 and postscript of January 13, 1838 in F. List, *Werke*, Vol. IV, pp. 47-8.
14. F. List to J.G. Cotta, September 6, 1838 in the List Archives (Reutlingen): printed in F. List, *Werke*, Vol. IV, p. 20.
15. Edgar Salin and Artur Sommer in F. List, *Werke*, Vol. IV, p. 20.
16. See chapter 12 below.
17. Charles Dupin, *Situation Progressive des Forces de la France depuis 1827* (Paris, 1827). In a speech in Philadelphia on November 3, 1827 List had referred to this book as an "excellent production", written by a "celebrated scholar".
18. T.H. Von Laue, *Sergei Witte and the Industrialisation of Russia* (1963), p. 57.
19. E.F. Heckscher, *The Continental System* (1922), p. 314.
20. E.F. Heckscher, *The Continental System* (1922), p. 322. For Germany's foreign trade between 1789 and 1834 see Martin Kutz, *Deutschlands Aussenhandel von der französischen Revolution bis zur Gründung des Zollvereins* (1974).
21. T.S. Ashton, *An Economic History of England. The Eighteenth Century* (1955) and L.S. Pressnell, "The Rate of Interest in the Eighteenth Century" in L.S. Pressnell (ed), *Studies in the Industrial Revolution* (presented to T.S. Ashton) (1960), pp. 178-214.
22. See below, chapter 1.
23. Adam Smith, *An Inquiry into the Nature and Causes of the Wealth of Nations*, 1776 (Everyman edition), Vol. I, p. 408.
24. J. Shield Nicholson's introduction of 1904 to F. List, *The National System of Political Economy*, 1841 (new edition, 1966), p. 448.

FRIEDRICH LIST

THE NATURAL SYSTEM OF POLITICAL ECONOMY 1837

Et la patrie, et l'humanité

Answer to the Question posed by the French Academy of Moral and Economic Sciences.

If a country proposes to introduce free trade or to modify its tariff, what factors should it take into account so as to reconcile in the fairest manner the interests of producers with those of consumers?

LIST'S INTRODUCTION

IN THE SCIENCE of economics, theory and practice are virtually divorced from one another – to the detriment of both. Economists condemn practical men as mere followers of routine who fail to appreciate either the truth or the grandeur of the doctrines enunciated by economists. Practical men, on the other hand, regard economists as mere doctrinaires who ignore the facts of life and inhabit a dream world of economic theories that exists only in their imagination.

Consequently the science of economics has failed to achieve its noblest aim which should be to elucidate economic practices and to show how they can be improved. And for their part practical men have not changed since they are as much children of routine today as they always have been in the past.

It is therefore certain that, in a more perfect world, economists would enunciate correct, reasonable and useful rules for practical men to fellow, while practical men would provide economists with facts and results which would confirm their theories and enable them to discover new doctrines.

Anyone who is both an economist and a practical man cannot deny that errors have been committed by both parties. Up to the present day all founders of new schools of economic thought and their disciples have failed to pay sufficient attention to experience gained in the world of affairs – experience which can be confirmed by all who have been engaged in practical activities. Economists have been overconfident concerning the conclusions of their reasoning – doubtless profound but the fruits of labours in the solitude of their studies – even when their conclusions are at variance with what people have always accepted as wise and correct. Even the worthy Adam Smith does not hesitate to brand as "an insidious and crafty animal" anyone who challenges his illusionary theories by practical experience.[1] And the French disciples and interpreters of this famous writer use equally opprobrious language when referring to practical men of affairs. Yet at all times in advanced nations there have been a great many men of affairs whose intelligence, experience, understanding and patriotism have earned them recognition as great leaders by their contemporaries. Can any impartial person doubt the value of their services or argue that men of this calibre have throughout the centuries played the part of idiots or fools?

On the other hand it must be admitted that, on the whole, practical men have been too ready to assess and to judge economic problems solely from their own point of view. They have scorned to make a thorough study of economic doctrines which would enable them to expose the errors of economists and to marshal the arguments with which they could refute the theorists on their own ground.

These assertions can be proved by taking as an example a French writer[2] who combines theoretical knowledge with practical experience. His observations have often led to striking conclusions. Unfortunately his arguments are based upon principles which have long been shown to be erroneous.

There are three reasons why men in public life, who shoulder great responsibilities, are justified in rejecting the principles laid down by doctrinaire writers which are obviously incompatible with experience in everyday life.

1. A great many economic doctrines have been put forward and the author of the newest theory always denounces the ideas of his predecessors as inadequate and erroneous.
2. Since Colbert's day no one has succeeded in putting a new economic doctrine into practice.
3. Economists never agree among themselves.[3]

1. [The "insidious and crafty animal" condemned by Adam Smith was the "statesman or politician whose councils are directed by the monetary fluctuations of affairs" (Adam Smith, *The Wealth of Nations*, ed. E. Cannan, 2 vols., 1904, Vol. I, p. 432).] [The editor's notes are in square brackets throughout.]

2. M. Ferrier. [François Louis Auguste Ferrier was the director of customs at Dunkirk. His major works were: *Du governement considéré dans ses rapports avec le commerce* (Paris, 1805) and *Du système maritime et commercial de l'Angleterre au XIX siècle (Paris, 1829)*.]

3. See the differences between the doctrines of J.B. Say and Adam Smith [p.21 below].

Thus the physiocrats proved the theories of the mercantilists to be untenable and then Adam Smith and J. B. Say exposed the inadequacies and errors of the physiocrats. In the United States two attempts to introduce free trade have failed. In France the treaties which Turgot concluded in the hope of moving as far as possible in the direction of free trade did not promote the welfare of the country but had exactly the opposite result. Germany has always followed the doctrine of free trade but far from deriving any benefit from this policy she has seen the collapse of the greater part of her productive powers.

Unfortunately the consequences of experiments made by doctrinaire economists are as uncertain as some of the results of medical experiments although in both cases the most recent theories have been put into practice. Whenever theoretical principles deviate from sound common sense and are opposed to what has been accepted as judicious, necessary and useful, it is prudent to refrain from taking any action which might be harmful to the welfare of society. It would be prudent to assume that the economic doctrine might be wrong and to delay making any hazardous changes until further research has either proved or disproved the validity of the theory.

This is certainly true of the so called doctrine of free trade which has been fashionable since Quesnay's day. In the name of scientific progress doctrinaire economists have urged practical men to adopt the policy of free trade without even explaining clearly what the doctrine means. Yet in all countries, practical men faced with real problems have always found it both necessary and judicious to regulate commerce and to restrict trade in various ways.

Whenever a number of enlightened, experienced, and intelligent men of affairs are faced with a problem that does not affect their private interests and are satisfied that a particular course of action is both necessary and desirable then one may presume that their decision is based upon common sense. This is true even if their action is condemned as unreasonable and contrary to the very nature of things by people who enjoy the reputation of being clever and well educated but who lack any experience of practical affairs.

Attention may be drawn to two ways in which even the most judicious proposals for economic reform are received by the public. First, such proposals nearly always have to face prejudiced opposition from conservative people who act by rule of thumb. Secondly, the reception of a new doctrine may be seriously hampered because it may be accepted and achieve popularity owing to its apparent simplicity – yet a great many of its supporters (lacking reasoning powers and hoping to be looked upon as knowledgeable people) will embrace the new theory without proof and without thought, so as to bask in the reflected glory of the originator of the doctrine. Thus the influence for good of the greatest reformers is to some extent counterbalanced by the fact that their errors gain popular acceptance as quickly as the truths which they have enunciated. Consequently the greater the skill with which a new and victorious doctrine is launched, the greater its apparent simplicity, and the greater the confidence that it inspires in men of knowledge and integrity, the more likely will it be that a critic will fail if he undertakes the difficult task of trying to draw attention to the errors of the theory. In many respects that is the position of the author of this treatise.

Although the writer fully acknowledges the great services that Adam Smith and J. B. Say have rendered, he believes that in order to answer the question posed by the Academy in a satisfactory manner, he must prove (i) that there are important deficiencies in the doctrines of these two great economists, (ii) that these deficiencies explain the incompatibility between the theory and practice of economics as well as the disputes between theorists and practical men, and (iii) that the truth lies somewhere between the dominant theory of free trade, and the normal commercial practice of the present day.

The writer appreciates the difficulty of the task that he has undertaken, since he himself acknowledges the exalted genius of the economists whom he presumes to criticise and he recognises that their doctrines have been accepted by many men of superior talents. Far from confident of his own abilities, he might hesitate to attempt such a difficult task were it not for his conviction that the Academy of Moral and Economic Sciences – by the form of the question it poses and by the advice given to competitors – apparently assumes that the doctrines of Adam Smith and J. B. Say are capable of being put into practice successfully.

In fact the history of all new ideas shows that human progress is not promoted by the uncritical acceptance of the doctrines of great thinkers. Such an attitude makes it impossible for their successors even to make good the deficiencies that occur in the writings of these great men. With the passage of time, however, intelligent people everywhere are prepared to accept the fact that it is right for the doctrines of profound thinkers of the past to be completed and improved by their successors.[1]

However, since the writer is both an economist and a man of affairs he enjoys certain advantages which may make up for his intellectual limitations. For many years he has not only studied the doctrines of the various schools of economic thought but he has also examined the actual facts of life. He has visited all the advanced countries in the world and he has studied their trade, industry, finances, and agriculture.

The widest possible gulf separates the men of theory from the men of practice when it comes to discussing the question of free trade.

The doctrine of free trade was first advocated by Quesnay and his disciples, the Physiocrats. Their arguments were based

1. [List's note] My doubts concerning the infallibility of economic doctrines and my right to pass judgment even on the past distinguished masters of this branch of knowledge have been strengthened by reading what the leaders of various schools of economic thought have had to say about each other. J. B. Say calls the Encyclopaedists dreamers – and dreamers indeed they are. He attacks their inspired assertions, their sectarian spirit, and their dogmatic and abstract language.

Consequently the supporters of today's dominant free trade doctrines have no cause whatever to complain of criticisms of their basic ideas. J. B. Say has opposed Adam Smith as vigorously as he has opposed the Encyclopaedists. Granted that in general he shows the dominant school of economic thought the respect it deserves, he nevertheless has no hesitation in attacking particular aspects of Adam Smith's doctrines. Say alleges that Adam Smith does not lay sufficient emphasis on the rôle of agriculture and capital; and that he actually exaggerates the significance of the division of labour – a principle which he was the first to discover. Say declares that Adam Smith places too much emphasis on labour as the main source of wealth. Say regards this point of view as too narrow and argues that Adam Smith should write "industry" instead of "labour." Say complains that Adam Smith gives no general account of the way in which wealth is divided. He considers that this aspect of economic theory has not yet been adequately explored. In short Say argues that Adam Smith's fundamental principles have not been proved. Say accuses Adam Smith of failing to make his position clear. Nevertheless, according to the introduction of Say's *Discours préliminaire,* while Adam Smith lays down "the most reasonable fundamental principles of economics" at the same time there is much confusion of thought in his book. There are plenty of accurate theories mixed up with positive facts. The uninitiated reader of Say's work really does not know what to think of so distinguished an economist as Adam Smith.

Consequently in France those whose opinion carries considerable weight have hardly felt able to support (any one of the) various rival economic doctrines. Charles Dupin, for example, writes: "I do not claim to have invented any economic doctrines or theories. I am not so foolish as to expect my countrymen to be taken in by my rambling speculations".

21

upon cosmopolitan principles. They put forward three propositions which are obviously erroneous and untenable – first that only agriculture produces wealth; secondly, that industry needs no protection; and thirdly that agriculture can flourish only if commerce is free from all restrictions.

Adam Smith reached the same conclusion by a different process of reasoning. He declared that the way to give the economy the most powerful stimulus was to leave it alone. Agricultural and industrial production and commerce should be left to private enterprise. Government intervention would only guide industry and capital into less profitable channels. Adam Smith considered that if a government wishes to increase national prosperity it has only to free production and foreign trade from all restrictions. He recommended that internal peace should be established as well as security for commerce and transport in order to secure the maximum welfare of a state. He believed that every nation possessed particular advantages, which would be fully exploited only if world free trade were established. He considered that exports were always balanced by imports of equal value and that there was no difference between trade in specie and trade in anything else. Adam Smith argued that Britain had become wealthy and powerful in spite of – and not because of – her restrictive commercial policy. He argued that import duties created privileges and monopolies which benefited particular groups of people but damaged the interests of consumers and of society as a whole. He denounced the levying of retaliatory import duties directed against the tariffs of other countries since such a policy harmed the country imposing the duties as much as the country that they were supposed to injure.

In view of these considerations Adam Smith, his disciples, and his successors have denounced every prohibition, every restriction, and every high import or export duty imposed to protect industry. They admit that, in present circumstances, the immediate total abolition of all commercial restrictions is impossible, but they urge the gradual removal of such restrictions. Merchants all over the world think only of their own private interests and agree with the theorists who advocate free trade but they make no effort to examine the validity of the arguments put forward in support of this fiscal policy. Since the profits of merchants come simply from exchanging products, they regard all imposts and restrictions as bad for business and they have invented and given their allegiance to the motto:

"laissez faire et laissez passer" – except for shipowners who consider bounties and privileges to be essential for merchant shipping and the fishing industry because – so they say – there can be no navy without a mercantile marine.

Those who earn salaries or draw pensions adopt the same attitude since it is in their interest to buy what they require in the cheapest market.

Manufacturers have very different ideas from farmers concerning free trade. Industrialists consider that freedom of commerce is desirable in foodstuffs, fuel, and raw materials because the lower the cost of these commodities, the better they are able to compete successfully with foreign rivals both at home and abroad. It is, however, difficult to satisfy the demands of manufacturers because there are so many definitions of what constitute "raw materials."

Farmers on the other hand consider that the welfare of society is seriously injured by every prohibition or restriction which increases the cost of manufactured goods. At the same time they argue that it is necessary to erect tariff walls to restrict the importation of foodstuffs. They put forward a thousand reasons to justify this demand. They declare that they pay higher wages and are burdened by higher taxes than their foreign competitors.

All governments are under conflicting pressures from these opposing interests. On the one hand they may favour greater freedom of trade yet at the same time they will realise the necessity of preserving and protecting existing interests so as to avoid any violent convulsion which might endanger the finances, credit or security of the state.

However enthusiastically they may pay lip service to the profundity of the doctrine of free trade, all governments recognise that it is much easier to declare their determination to establish free trade than it is to adopt a policy that will overcome all the difficulties and will achieve the object that they have in mind. They have neither the time not the desire to make a detailed examination of the doctrine of free trade and they are continually distracted by the demands of various pressure groups and by the actual situation in which the country finds itself. Faced with such an awkward and embarrassing situation it is quite natural that governments should take the easiest course open to them to surmount the difficulties with which they are beset. This accounts for the great gulf which separates their words from their deeds.

In England, where the free trade doctrine was born and received the greatest support, a recent attempt to put the theory into practice failed. After the advantages and drawbacks had been carefully weighed, it was decided to leave things as they were. It was evident that the claims of the supporters of free trade were unfounded.

What did the great champions of free trade – men like Canning and Huskisson – ever do to put into practice the doctrine which they so fervently supported? They caused a few laws to be passed which proved to be useless and are already a dead letter. They reduced a few import duties but always took care that the new duties were high enough to safeguard the home market for English manufacturers. They lowered unnecessarily high tariff walls but always made sure that import duties remained high enough to protect the country from a flood of imports. When they abolished some prohibitions they replaced them with import duties high enough to be equivalent to a prohibition. They even dealt with the Corn Laws in this way although the abolition of the import duties on cereals would have been of great benefit to their country. Did they ever do anything to reduce import duties on the products which France, Germany, or Switzerland would like to sell in the English market? No, they did not.

These men actually proclaimed that they had taken a great step forward towards free trade. But their hypocrisy was obvious since their true purpose was simply to trick those countries into making tariff concessions on the English goods which they imported. Even (the United States), the world's youngest state, which has applied the most modern principles and inventions of our age to achieve unparalleled economic growth, has not been able to adopt the policy of free trade.

Sensible impartial observers have to admit that although England preaches free trade, she practises something very different. What England means by free trade is the right to sell freely all over the world both her own manufactured goods and the produce of her colonies while at the same time she erects hostile tariff barriers to prevent foreign goods from competing with her own products in the home market. It must in fairness be admitted that the way in which England treats the rest of the world is no different from the way in which other nations treat their weaker neighbours who are in no position to retaliate.

There is therefore a real danger that the strongest nations will use the motto "Free Trade" as an excuse to adopt a policy which will certainly enable them to dominate the trade and industry of weaker countries and reduce them to a condition of slavery.[1]

All over the world people misuse the term "Free Trade". They use it to deceive people while lining their own pockets under the cloak of patriotism. The vast mass of humanity cannot be expected to grasp the full implications of high politics or the differences between commercial, political, and social freedom.

Inside a country the policy of free trade is beneficial provided that it simply means that citizens are free to manufacture what they please and are not restricted when moving their produce from one place to another. But free trade in foreign commerce is far from beneficial. Indeed it is the equivalent of commercial slavery. Free trade in this sense – if introduced unilaterally – permits foreign competitors to ruin native industry while denying to native manufacturers the right to compete on equal terms with foreign rivals in markets abroad. Such "freedom" leaves us to the tender mercies of foreigners. Our industry and commerce are dependent upon their laws and regulations.

To answer satisfactorily the question posed by the Academy it will be necessary, first of all, to recommend certain changes which will reform both the theory and the practice of economics.

---

1. [List's note] Montesquieu in his *Esprit des Lois* writes: "Free trade is not a licence granted to merchants to do as they please. It is a servitude imposed upon them. If the state imposes restrictions upon the individual merchant, it does so in the interest of commerce in general. Trade is never subjected to greater restrictions than in free nations, and it is never subjected to fewer restrictions than in nations under despotic governments." And again: "England restricts the individual merchant but promotes commerce in general."

CHAPTER ONE

Cosmopolitan Economics*

MAN HAS TO WREST from nature what he requires to satisfy his needs. The more intelligence, integrity and capacity for hard work that he possesses, the better equipped will he be to achieve his ends. He can, however, achieve little on his own since both his powers and the area in which he can operate are very limited. He needs the support of his own kind to supplement his modest powers and the restricted resources at his disposal. The greater the number of his associates – and the greater their intelligence, integrity, and capacity for hard work – the easier will it be for him to achieve his aim.

By means of the reciprocal exchange of goods and services, each individual can concentrate his efforts on the occupation for which he is best fitted by his physical and intellectual qualities, by his education, by his experience, and by the natural resources at his disposal. In this way the output of each individual reaches the maximum that his abilities permit and the surplus goods that he makes can be exchanged for the greatest quantity of goods produced by others. This is called the division of labour.

The greater the growth of the productive powers of society, the greater the area in which they can operate, and the greater the number of producers, the greater is the number and variety of the goods that can be made and which are available to each individual. As the economy expands, so each individual can produce more goods which he can exchange for foreign goods. In this way he can become progressively richer. But the first and the main condition for the production of wealth is the existence of complete freedom for the individual to produce goods and to exchange them.

If the inhabitants of a town, a group of towns, or a number of provinces are able to exchange goods freely among themselves, their standard of living will improve in a way that would not be possible if the movement of goods were restricted by imposts

*[Or Individual and Social Economics]

27

or prohibitions. Similarly the wealth of the various nations in the world would reach a maximum if universal freedom of trade were established.

In certain circumstances there may be a failure to balance the various goods produced by various individuals. This may occur because of the freedom of the individual to engage in whatever economic activity he pleases, to produce as many goods as he sees fit, and to make what he regards as the most profitable bargain when he exchanges the goods that he has made. The individual does not know if too many or too few competitors have decided to produce the same goods as himself, and he cannot judge if the demand for his goods is rising or falling. The best way of restoring the balance between supply and demand which has been disturbed in this way, is to establish the greatest possible freedom of trade between all the countries in the world.

If agricultural and manufacturing products can be freely exchanged they will be made in those places designed by nature for their production. The state of farming, the availability of scientific and technical knowledge and the social and political condition of the inhabitants are all factors which will stimulate economic growth. The fullest development of manufacturing industry, however, will take place only when various branches of industry are so intimately linked that one process can follow another as closely as possible. The principle of co-operation is as indispensable to steady regular industrial growth as the principle of the division of labour.

Experience teaches us that a high degree of civilisation, and the labours of successive generations, are necessary to bring the industrial capacity of a country to a high degree of perfection. To achieve this object a regular – though perhaps a slow – rate of growth both of output and of sales must have first priority. Any step backwards must be avoided at all costs.

Particular countries may achieve an overwhelming industrial ascendancy owing to the special aptitudes of the inhabitants, the introduction of improvements in the manufacturing processes, or to natural advantages. In brief the advantages bestowed by nature or by history may enable a country to become – and to remain – a great industrial power. Such a country will be able to supply the world with the best goods at the lowest prices. And in this way the manufacturing power of the whole world will quickly reach hitherto unimagined heights to the advantage of all humanity.

At the same time the economic progress of the agrarian countries will expand in the most natural and sensible manner. Their prosperity will grow as they sell their raw materials and agricultural products to industrial countries while they can buy the manufactured products, the tools, and the most efficient machines that they require. Their increased wealth and their contacts with industrial countries will enable them to improve their political and social institutions. The time will come when these agrarian states will themselves become manufacturing countries. Moreover the surplus capital and workers in the industrial states will inevitably move to agrarian countries when they are ripe for industrial development.

As each country prospers and becomes more civilised it acquires an aptitude for the manufacturing arts and in due course it will become an industrial state.

For this prosperity to be procured by every nation and by the whole human race it is necessary to have universal peace. Conflicts between nations – whether settled by force of arms or by other means – must be replaced by an alliance of all peoples governed by laws of universal application. A world republic, as envisaged by J. B. Say, is necessary to secure the fulfilment of the dreams of the free traders.

─────────────

CHAPTER TWO

National Economics*

IN THE PREVIOUS chapter we summarised the main features of the most widely accepted economic doctrine of our time. This doctrine is clearly concerned only with individuals and with a universal republic embracing all members of the human race. But this doctrine omits a vital intermediate stage between the individual and the whole world. This is the nation, to which its members are united by the tie of patriotism.

*[Or Political Economy]

At present the world is divided into a number of different states, each with its particular national characteristics. Each individual – be he a manufacturer, farmer, merchant, professional man, or pensioner – is a member of the country in which he lives. The state protects him and helps him to achieve the aims that he pursues as an individual.

Individuals owe to a nation their culture, their language, their opportunity to work, and the safety of their property. Above all they depend upon the state in their relations with people in other countries. They share in the nation's glory and in its misfortunes; they share in its memories of the past and its hopes for the future; they share its wealth and its poverty. From the nation they draw all the benefits of civilisation, enlightenment, progress, and social and political institutions, as well as advances in the arts and sciences. If a nation declines, the individual shares in the disastrous consequences of its fall.

So it is right and proper that the individual should be prepared to sacrifice his own interests for the benefit of the nation to which he belongs.

As yet no universal republic exists. What is called "international law" is, for the time being, only the embryo of a future world state. Common sense and – as we saw in our first chapter – mutual interests should induce nations to abate their natural envy and their distrust of each other. Common sense tells us that war between nations is as stupid and savage as duels between individuals. Mutual interests would suggest the establishment of perpetual peace as well as free trade between nations which would bring the greatest prosperity to us all. Nevertheless it is not yet safe for the lamb to lie down with with lion.

So far there are only a few people, even in the most enlightened countries, who have grasped the fact that perpetual peace and universal free trade are both desirable and necessary. Nations have not yet attained a state of political and social development which would make such a reform possible. Moreover the civilised and enlightened countries in the world cannot be expected to disarm and to renounce warfare so long as there are in existence powers which reject the ideas of peaceful prosperity for the whole human race and are bent upon conquering and enslaving other nations.

Just as the discovery of gunpowder enabled states to establish law and order in their towns and in isolated regions so it now seems that only some new (and so far unknown) invention will persuade people of the possibility – indeed the necessity – of establishing a system of laws which will enable them to live together in peace throughout the world.

At present a nation may be regarded from two distinct points of view with regard to its relations with other countries:

(i) First, a nation is a sovereign political body. Its destiny is to safeguard and to maintain its independence by its own efforts. Its duty is to preserve and to develop its prosperity, culture, nationality, language, and freedom – in short, its entire social and political position in the world.

(ii) Secondly, a nation is a branch of human society. It is the duty of a nation – as far as its own special interests permit – to join with other countries in the task of promoting the welfare and prosperity of the whole world.

Regarded from the first point of view a nation should adopt an independent "national economy". Regarded from the second point of view it should adopt a "cosmopolitan economy". An analogy between the "national" and the "cosmopolitan" economics would be the two kinds of legal system which exist in the world. There are "national" systems of law which are in force in particular countries and there is a "cosmopolitan" – or international – system of law which is in force all over the world.

Cosmopolitan economics – or universal free trade between all the countries in the world – is only in the very earliest stage of development. Nations can only move slowly, step by step, towards the attainment of world free trade. They can do so only insofar as it is advantageous and not disadvantageous for them to adopt such a policy.

A nation which dismantled its fortresses and demobilised its armed forces would not enjoy the benefits of eternal peace, despite the fact that our religion teaches us to love and to help one another. Similarly a nation which abolished its import duties while other countries retained their tariffs, would not enjoy the benefits of world free trade.

The doctrine of national economics teaches us that a country which hopes to attain the highest degree of independence, culture and material prosperity, should adopt every measure within its power to defend its economic security from any foreign attack,

31

whether such an attack takes the form of hostile legislation or military action. To enable a country to protect itself it is essential that it should establish industries and foster their development – insofar as this is possible with available physical and human resources.

The foundations upon which national independence can be built are quite inadequate without the development of industries. A country of farmers and peasants can never maintain the military power – or the human and physical means to defend itself – that can be maintained by an industrialised country. The position of an agrarian country is worsened by the fact that just when it needs to defend itself it may be unable to find markets for its agricultural products and it may thus be deprived of the capital with which to create new industries. Moreover those of its merchants who live abroad – men who are half foreigners already – will in wartime never be such sound patriots as manufacturers and farmers whose entire livelihood depends upon the maintenance of their country's independence.

In time of war every country is forced to establish factories to make those goods which were formerly imported from abroad in exchange for products made at home. The result is the same as that achieved by a prohibitive fiscal policy in peace time. The nation is forced to demand great sacrifices from consumers in order to create new industries. And this happens just when the means available for the establishment of manufactures have been reduced to a minimum. If free trade is introduced when hostilities cease the newly established industries will be thrown to the tender mercies of foreign competitors. In these circumstances a country will lose all the capital, all the experience, and all the work of the war years and will return to its former position of weakness and dependence upon foreigners.

In the event of war or of the threat of war it is essential for a Great Power to establish industries. And in peacetime a government should foster the establishment of new branches of manufacture to safeguard the prosperity and the culture of the nation.

We saw in the previous chapter how the division of labour and the co-operation of productive powers follows automatically from the adoption of the policy of free trade. But if the natural growth of the economy is hindered by the hostile political actions of other states it would be foolish to expect that the same growth will take place that would have occurred if universal free trade existed. In such circumstances a nation can expect the industrial sector of the economy to grow only if defensive measures are taken through political action. If a country stimulates the establishment and the expansion of manufactures by adopting a suitable tariff it will promote the continued extension of the division of labour and a proper balance between agriculture and industry. Co-operation between industry and agriculture will stimulate the continued growth of the economy and will protect the country from any possibility of a slump.

From this point of view the imposition of a protective tariff in no way hampers the natural growth of the economy. The object of a tariff is to frustrate any hostile action by foreigners to harm a country's economy by political action or by acts of war. While achieving its immediate object a protective tariff will also foster the natural and normal expansion of home industries. A protective tariff establishes free trade within the frontiers of a single state, as an alternative to the establishment of universal free trade. In the world in which we live it is impossible to introduce universal free trade just now because the various nations into which it is divided are intent upon pursuing their own selfish economic interests.

In these circumstances one would fail to appreciate the nature of the relations between a state and the individuals who compose it if one were to argue that a national commercial policy designed to control trade with foreign countries could in any way prejudice the rights and interests of the individuals who form the nation. We have already observed that the fortunes or misfortunes of individuals are dependent upon the maintenance of the independence and progress of the whole nation. We have seen that each country can secure economic growth by means of a specially designed tariff. It is obvious therefore that individuals in a country must accept the restrictions imposed for the welfare of the nation as a whole. It is equally obvious that the freedom of the individual must be restricted to secure the freedom of all the individuals who make up a nation. In doing this a state acts in the same way as it does when it demands part of an individual's wealth to pay for the administration of the country or when it calls upon its citizens to serve in the armed forces, at risk of life and limb, to defend its independence.

CHAPTER THREE

Theory of Productive Powers

IN ORDER TO establish which economic principles should be used as guide lines for a national commercial system and for a tariff it is necessary to examine the economy of individuals. Two factors are involved. The first is the skill or the physical labour which enable something to be produced. The second is an object that has been produced which can be exchanged for something else and therefore has a value. Two different economic doctrines – cosmopolitan and national economics – are both based upon a recognition of the existence of these factors. The doctrines are derived from different principles but they have numerous points in common.[1]

A few examples may be given to illustrate the difference between the two doctrines. A father who spends his savings to give his

1.[Note by List] J.B. Say almost certainly appreciates the significance of an independent theory of productive powers but he does not make a clear distinction between the two doctrines which we have mentioned. In his first book (*Nouveau principe d'économie politique*, chapter 2) he distinguishes between what he calls "high politics" and "political economy". He writes: "The first is concerned with cultural needs, the second with material needs". It is only in his second book (*Traité d'économie politique*) that Say includes "cultural production" in his doctrine under the general heading of "immaterial goods" and "immaterial industry". But he does not regard "cultural production" simply as a factor in the production of material goods. In his last book (*Économie politique pratique*, Vol. I, p. 211) Say writes: "When intellectual services are rendered they are an immaterial product which has value and is an object of exchange. It is always an application of human knowledge to material human needs". Say argues that "cultural production" does not create productive powers but does aid in the production of material goods. Baron Charles Dupin in his famous book *Les forces productives de la France* was the first to recognise fully the significance of productive powers. He emphasises the real practical value of productive powers. In an appendix to Dupin's book J. Droz (Book IV, chapter 4) writes: "I have observed with regret that several writers have employed expressions which apparently imply that all our needs are of a material character". This emphasis on material things has gone so far that Thomas Cooper, a distinguished American economist, evaluates human beings by the money spent on their education. Thus he declares that a lawyer is worth 3,000 or 4,000 dollars. Even Droz has tried to prove that there is a connection between productive powers and the theory of value. He quotes the example that we have cited from Cooper to show that a father sacrifices "value" to gain "productive power" when he pays for his son's education.

children a good education sacrifices "value" but substantially increases the productive powers of the next generation. But a father who invests his savings and neglects to educate his children increases the "exchange value" at his disposal by spending the interest on his capital at the expense of the future productive powers of the country. According to the doctrine of productive powers a father or a teacher who trains the citizens of the future is a producer, but according to the theory of value he is simply a consumer. A planter, who raises slaves, is "productive" in the sense that he increases the wealth of the nation, but he weakens the productive powers of the state. There are many products, such as alcoholic liquors, which increase the "exchange value" of a nation but weaken its productive powers.

Just as it is possible to sacrifice productive power to gain "exchange value" so it is possible to give up "exchange value" to increase productive power. The result of giving up "exchange value" for greater productive power is not immediately apparent but it is seen in the increased output of the next generation or even later generations.

The owner of a large estate will sacrifice significant "exchange value" if he decides that his son should not work on his farms to increase their output but should travel abroad to study new farming methods and to bring home new plants, seeds and improved livestock. Here the immediate loss is balanced by an improvement in the productive power achieved by later generations rather than by the landowner himself.

While Watt and Arkwright were inventing new machines and improving them there was a loss of "exchange value" but eventually these pioneers enormously increased the productive power not only of England but of the whole world. Most inventors and those who advance technical knowledge sacrifice their savings but the national economy is immensely strengthened. Countries, such as the United States of America, have suffered huge economic losses to achieve political independence but their sacrifices have ultimately been rewarded by an immense increase in their prosperity and productive power.

A nation which has an agrarian economy and is dependent upon foreign countries (for its manufactured goods) can – if it has the necessary moral qualities or natural advantages – stimulate the establishment of industries by means of a protective tariff. Such a country may well sacrifice much "exchange value" for the moment if its new workshops produce expensive goods of poor quality. But it will greatly increase its productive power in the future because it has fostered the division of labour on a large scale and has ensured the permanent co-operation between farming and industry. In this way the national economy will grow and the welfare of the people will increase.

This is our main argument in support of a protective tariff and in opposition to the doctrine of free trade. We shall (in the following chapters) see how doctrinaire free traders have confused two quite different economic doctrines in their specious arguments to discredit those who favour protective tariffs.

The theory of productive power not only explains why a protective system is necessary but also shows how a tariff should be applied. Import duties should not be levied for revenue purposes because this might seriously injure the nation's productive forces. To raise money for the state should be only a secondary object of a tariff. Again import duties should not be levied in the hope of enticing specie into the country – and of keeping it there. This is a discredited aspect of the mercantile system. Such a policy might weaken rather than strengthen the country's productive power.

Import duties should be levied to protect and gradually to increase the nation's productive power. With this object in mind the rates of duty levied under a tariff should be adapted to the needs of a particular country. This will be discussed at greater length in our fifth chapter.

CHAPTER FOUR

Theory of Value[1]

J.R.McCULLOCH, the most distinguished contemporary English economist,[2] has rightly given the name "theory of value" to a

1. [List's note to this chapter, written when the treatise was finished, is printed in an appendix; see below, pp. 193-5.]
2. J..R. McCulloch (1789-1864) was a contributor to the *Edinburgh Review*, Professor of Political Economy at University College, London and Comptroller of

doctrine based upon the teachings of Adam Smith and J.B. Say. The latter clearly included the theory of value in his definition of "political economy" which, in his view, was that branch of know-ledge which examines the production, division, and consumption of wealth. But this definition shows that Say does not propose to discuss how productive power is established, how they develop, or how they can be destroyed.

We do not deny that Adam Smith and J.B. Say recognise the significance of productive power for the creation of material wealth. But we hope to show that they have failed to recognise the difference not only between the two doctrines which we have mentioned but also between the theories of cosmopolitan and national economics. These writers confuse the two theories, and when they seek to support the policy of free trade they are quite capable of using propositions derived from one doctrine as arguments against the other doctrine.

Moreover Adam Smith, more logical than J.B. Say, classes as unproductive those who – like professors, teachers, judges, artists and actors – do not produce any material wealth. This is fully justified if one considers the theory of value in isolation. But if one appreciates how the work of these members of society contributes to the growth of a nation's productive power one can see that they are really more productive than those who make material goods. The judge upholds the safety of the individual and the sanctity of property, the teacher prepares the way for the future extension of learning, including technical knowledge, while the artist establishes and elevates the culture of society.

Say does appreciate, though only in a vague sort of way, the existence of this important lacuna in his doctrine and he regards these creators of productive forces as mere producers of cultural (or immaterial) values. Since his doctrine is entirely materialistic in conception – he is concerned only with the "exchange value" of material goods – he tries to justify his view by defining the activities of these producers in purely materialistic terms. Say argues that these producers create only "immaterial values" which are con-sumed as soon as they are made. If this were really the case the producers in question would be engaged in a truly empty sort of

H.M. Stationery Office. His books include *Principles of Political Economy* (1820), *The Rate of Wages* (1826), *Dictionary of Commerce* (1832) and *Statistical Account of the British Empire* (1837).

production which would hardly be worth discussing at all. Say also argues that the producers of "cultural values" receive "exchange values" for their services. This argument, too, falls to the ground since it implies that the producers of "cultural values" make no contribution to the wealth of the nation.

The foundation of Say's doctrine is the conception of material wealth. His whole system is based upon it. Consequently he concentrates his attention upon the theory of value and he is interested in productive forces only insofar as they can be brought into direct association with his doctrine.

On the other hand Say's assessment of foreign commerce and import duties would unquestionably have been quite different if he had distinguished clearly between cosmopolitan and national economics, if he had given the theory of productive power priority over the theory of value, and if he had considered the theory of value only insofar as material wealth creates things that contribute to future economic expansion.

When Say denounces import duties and suggests that they fail to stimulate industrial progress, he uses arguments which are valid only as criticisms of the mercantile system and which are all dependent upon his theory of value. He thinks that every nation should buy the goods that it requires in the cheapest market. He believes that it is as absurd for a nation as for an individual to manufacture goods at a higher cost than they can be purchased from foreigners. This is obviously an argument which applies only to a merchant who makes a living by exchanging goods or "exchange values". A merchant is not concerned with the theory of productive power and may indeed be ignorant of its very existence. And Say's argument is not even sound when applied to private individuals for they should always aim at the preservation and growth of their own personal productive power.

Above all we must point out that Say mentions only the immediate sacrifices that the consumer has to make when import duties are imposed. He fails to consider the long term advantages of a policy of protection. If it were always foolish to make short term sacrifices for long term gains it would be a mistake to plant pear trees and sensible to buy pears since the cost of planting trees is so high that every pear picked at the end of the first year would be more expensive than a basket of pears bought in the market. To this sort of doctrinaire argument a practical farmer would reply that he does not plant a tree to reap the crop that it will bear at the end of the first year. He plants a tree to gather the pears that it will bear for a hundred years. The cost of planting a tree should be compared with the fruit that it will bear throughout its life. And a nation establishes industries not for a hundred years but for the whole period of its existence. Moreover the indirect advantages that agriculture derives from the establishment of industries are an additional bonus to the direct advantages gained by society from the growth of the manufacturing sector of the economy. Finally, a nation should not regard the progress of industries from a purely economic point of view. Manufactures become a very important part of the nation's political and cultural heritage.

A further weakness of Say's argument is that he assumes that a country which has – for one or more years – had enough money to pay for the goods which it buys more cheaply abroad than they can be manufactured at home, will always be in a financial position to make such purchases.

Say makes another erroneous statement which we shall discuss in more detail later. He asserts that import duties upon manufactured goods confer upon industrialists a monopoly at the expense of farmers and consumers in general. In fact the monopoly is not one granted to a particular set of individuals at the expense of another group of individuals. It is a monopoly granted to the country as a whole at the expense of foreigners. The long term results of the protection of industry by import duties are as follows. Assuming that people are free to choose their occupation and to move from one job to another; assuming the existence of universal education; assuming the availability of adequate capital in the country that has conferred a monopoly upon itself by a protective tariff – then in the long run native manufacturers will be able to produce goods which can be sold at lower prices than those charged for foreign products. For these reasons – and because of the advantages gained by farmers from a growing demand for their foodstuffs and raw materials – the initial high prices that consumers pay for native manufactured goods protected by a tariff are of minor consequence compared with the ultimate advantage of having a strong home industry.

We believe that we have drawn attention to the mistakes concerning import duties which Adam Smith and Say have made through confusing the theory of value with the theory of productive forces. We shall give further proofs later.

On the very first page of his book Say makes it clear how little he knows about the theory of productive power. He asserts that all nations are capable of becoming prosperous under any form of government. In fact a study of the history of all peoples at all times shows that the prosperity of a country depends to a great extent upon the nature of its political constitution.[1]

Say makes a still more extraordinary assertion when he argues that politics should have nothing to do with economics. This contradicts the very name of his doctrine. Since he calls his doctrine "political economy" it should be concerned as much with politics as wth economics. The way in which Adam Smith and J. B. Say both completely exclude politics from their doctrines is the clearest proof that they are concerned solely with the theories of cosmopolitan economics and value and not with the doctrine of national economics.

Adam Smith and J.B. Say have, of course, performed a very useful service as founders of the theory of cosmopolitan economics

1. [List's note] In his *Traité d'économie politique* (1824), *discours préliminaire*, Say writes: "Political science, which ought properly to be regarded as the study of the organisation of society, has long been confused with economics, which examines how the wealth which satisfies our needs is created, distributed, and consumed. The wealth of a country is really independent of its political organisation. A state will become rich if it is well administered, whatever its constitution may be. Nations ruled by absolute monarchs have prospered, while those governed by popular assemblies have seen their economies ruined. It is only indirectly that political liberty may be more favourable (than a dictatorship) to economic prosperity – or for that matter to the progress of cultural activities". All history refutes this notion. The truth is the very opposite. No nation has ever achieved success as an industrial power without also enjoying a high degree of political freedom. No country ruled by a despot has ever been able to establish manufactures on a large scale or to achieve economic prosperity. Free peoples have declined and have become poor and weak, but this has occurred only after they have lost their liberty. A despot has sometimes secured a certain degree of prosperity for his subjects but this has happened only if he had the good fortune to employ a number of exceptionally able ministers and officials. But, as the Emperor Alexander once remarked, that is only a fortunate chance. As soon as the services of able officials are no longer available the economy of the country declines. Liberty and industry are synonymous and cannot be separated. Only a strong democratic element in society can bring opulence to a monarchical or an aristocratic state. The nobles of Venice committed suicide as soon as they effectively weakened the democratic element in the city state. Industry demands a democratic government which pursues the same economic policy for many hundreds of years.

The validity of this proposition is supported not only by historical evidence but also by no less an authority than Montesquieu who writes in his *Esprit des lois* (Part II, p. 192): "In a servile state people work to preserve what they have got rather than to increase their wealth. In a free society people work to acquire riches rather than to preserve wealth".

and the theory of value. Their fame is not lessened by their failure to remedy certain gaps in their doctrines, or by the fact that their mistake in confusing two different theories should have been repeated by their disciples, or by the continued contradiction between their theories and what happens in the real world of business.

Our thanks are due to Adam Smith and to Say because they have clearly laid down the principles of individual economics and cosmopolitan economics. These doctrines may be regarded as aims which nations should strive to achieve. But experience teaches us that Adam Smith and Say have not shown countries the right road to follow to achieve the noble ideal of world free trade. Their services are not diminished by the fact that – although they have developed the theory of value to its greatest extent – they have failed to appreciate the significance of the doctrine of productive power. And Adam Smith and Say have also attacked the policy of protection by mistaken arguments based upon erroneous principles.

We define the theory of value as those unalterable principles which can be shown to have existed unchanged among all peoples and at all times with regard to the level of prices, rents, profits, wages, supply and demand, capital, and interest. As a discussion of the theory of value does not fall within the scope of the question posed by the Academy we shall examine the doctrine only insofar as it touches upon our own doctrines of national economics and productive power.

CHAPTER FIVE

The Differences between Countries and their National Economies

SUPPORTERS OF THE doctrine of cosmopolitan economics do not consider it necessary to trouble themselves very much either with the economic situation in particular countries or with the way in which particular national economies can be improved. They simply wish to show that the maximum prosperity will be secured by the establishment of universal free trade in a world wide republic. They believe that nations can bring this about merely by abolishing all tariffs and by leaving individuals absolutely free to trade as they please.

From our point of view the problem is not so simple because we have to bring our doctrine of national economics into relationship with the actual situation in which particular states are placed. On approaching the problem we find that there are great differences between various nations. Some are civilised, some semi-civilised, and some are in a state of barbarism. There are giants and dwarfs among the states of the world. Some nations are strong while others are weak; some are enlightened while others are sunk in ignorance; some are industrious while others are lazy. Some countries are eager to adopt new ideas while others cling firmly to old established customs. Some nations enjoy liberty, some are only half-free, while others are enslaved. Some countries are skilful, some are not. Some nations are endowed with rich natural resources while others are entirely lacking in such resources. Some nations have only an agrarian sector of the economy, others have great industries and commercial activities, while others have developed an enviable balance between all aspects of economic activity. Do nature and common sense intend that one procrustean bed should accommodate all these different countries?

The lessons of history justify our opposition to the assertion that states reach economic maturity most rapidly if left to their own devices. A study of the origin of various branches of manufacture reveals that industrial growth may often have been due to chance. It may be chance that leads certain individuals to a particular place to foster the expansion of an industry that was once small and insignificant – just as seeds blown by chance by the wind may sometimes grow into big trees. But the growth of industries is a process that may take hundreds of years to complete and one should not ascribe to sheer chance what a nation has achieved through its laws and institutions. In England Edward III created the manufacture of woollen cloth and Elizabeth founded the mercantile marine and foreign trade. In France Colbert was responsible for all that a great power needs to develop its economy. Following these examples every responsible government should strive to remove those obstacles that hinder the progress of civilisation and should stimulate the growth of those economic forces that a nation carries in its bosom.

Sound laws and institutions and an efficient administration can abolish fanaticism, superstition, idleness, ignorance, and wastefulness. They can abolish privileges and harmful institutions. They can improve education, foster liberty, and raise moral standards. They can attract foreign skill and capital. They can create new economic resources for the benefit of the nation. Obviously a single individual, without the support of the state, could achieve little, if anything, on these lines by himself.

It would, for example, be foolish for a tiny state to introduce a tariff since its own resources would be neither large enough nor diverse enough for it to survive on its own. Its internal market would be too small to support industrial growth. But what a tiny state cannot accomplish in isolation it can accomplish in association with other countries. This has recently been proved by the establishment of the German customs union.[1] Prussia is a great power but its provinces are too scattered to enable it to establish an efficient system of tariffs, except in collaboration with smaller neighbours. Switzerland will never consider introducing a protective tariff[2] but the Swiss cantons are in a position to secure a substantial expansion of their productive forces in various ways. They can disseminate technical knowledge, improve internal communications, conclude commercial treaties with foreign countries, and set up trading companies.

The Kingdoms of Naples, Spain, and Portugal can stimulate the growth of their productive forces by extending facilities for education, by protecting persons and property, by improving agriculture and mining, by encouraging people to work harder, by improving political institutions, by attracting capital and skilled labour from abroad, and by exchanging what they can produce for foreign manufactured goods. All this would be much better than imposing high import duties.

The South American states are in much the same position. Their protective tariffs have had the very opposite effect than they would have had in countries with progressive, industrious and inventive

1. [The Zollverein was established in 1834.]
2. [At this time each Swiss canton had its own customs duties. The federal government secured control over tariffs in 1848.]

populations which (like those living in the United States) live under advanced social and political institutions. In South America protective tariffs cannot at a stroke turn an ignorant people into a well educated, industrious and inventive people. Only a few weak factories would be established in South America (under the shelter of a tariff) and they would produce only expensive goods of poor quality. No competition would develop at home to encourage the manufacture of better goods at a lower price. In these circumstances foreigners would hesitate to invest their capital and skill in backward South American states which cannot even provide adequate security for persons and property. And if, by chance, in exceptional circumstances, a foreigner would venture his capital and skill in South America his sole object would be to make his fortune as quickly as possible before returning to his native land.

In backward countries the growth of industries would harm rather than benefit agriculture because the manufactured goods which are produced would be poor in quality and high in price. Such industrial undertakings would not buy sufficient quantities of raw materials or foodstuffs to be of any real benefit to the agrarian sector of the economy. But if the government of a backward country were to stimulate the importation of cheap manufactured goods from abroad and the export of raw materials and foodstuffs to foreign states it will gradually stimulate the demand at home for a greater diversity of manufactured goods. And this will happen at the very time that the people are securing the means by which they can buy the manufactured goods that they require. In this way people will be encouraged to increase the output of their farms so as to be able to buy manufactured goods from abroad. This will provide a stimulus to people to work hard and to save their money. Educational facilities will be extended and better standards of morality will be established. Political institutions, too, will be improved. In this way a backward nation can develop into a progressive state.

In the United States, on the other hand, the position is different. The country has a well developed agrarian sector of the economy; rich natural resources; a large domestic market; a progressive, enlightened, inventive, skilled, and venturesome population; and a very efficient political constitution. In this country the introduction of a protective tariff has fostered the growth of important industries based upon machinery and using raw materials produced at home.

The progress of other branches of industry which are still operated by craftsmen – such as silk weaving – will not be so satisfactory so long as labour costs are higher than in other countries. The productive powers of the country would be stimulated if such goods were purchased from abroad and were paid for by exporting raw materials and foodstuffs.

In Russia there are factors which hamper the development of industries by means of a protective tariff. They are the backwardness of the country, the absence of political liberty and the lack of a middle class. It will be necessary to abolish serfdom and to encourage the development of a middle class by granting a measure of municipal self-government to the towns. Only when this has been done will the beneficial results of the tariff become evident.

The situation in France and in Belgium is quite different. These countries possess all the prerequisites, all the conditions, all the means, and all the powers which are needed to achieve the maximum degree of industrialisation. The obstacles which once hindered the growth of modern manufactures in France and Belgium have been virtually all removed. These countries have already made great progress in industrial development and they have only to hold on to what they have achieved to expand their manufactures still further. Compared with England, however, France and Belgium can be regarded as only industrial states of the second rank.

Germany has the ability and the natural resources to become a manufacturing country but there are numerous difficulties which still prevent the attainment of full industrialisation and these have still to be overcome. Since it is only quite recently that the establishment of the Zollverein has made possible the introduction of a uniform tariff[1] Germany is still well behind France and Belgium as far as industrial progress is concerned. Germany may be described as a manufacturing country of the third rank which has the ability to become a manufacturing country of the second rank.

We have shown that different nations have reached different stages in their development as industrial countries. Because of these differences, various countries will best be served by different types of protective tariffs.

1. [The Zollverein did not cover the whole of Germany when List was writing. The Tax Union (Hanover, Oldenburg, Brunswick), Hamburg, Bremen, Lübeck, Schleswig, Holstein, and the two Mecklenburgs had not yet joined the German customs union.]

CHAPTER SIX

The Dominant Nation

THE PRESENT position of England is obviously quite different from that of all other countries. England is far in advance of all her rivals with regard to her agriculture and industry, her fleet and overseas possessions, her national wealth, her exports and imports, her efficient means of communication. It may satisfy one's self-esteem to doubt England's superiority but it is neither profitable nor sensible for people in relatively backward countries to indulge in that sort of egotism. A failure to face obvious facts would prevent such countries from judging correctly their true situation when compared with that of England and it would blind them to the way in which England's industrial and commercial supremacy harms their own economic interests.

In England two developments occurred sooner than anywhere else. First, the middle classes have secured their freedom. Secondly, the monarchy, the aristocracy, and the bourgeoisie have united to pursue the common aim of expanding both the nation's productive powers and its trade in all parts of the world. Consequently farming, industry, and commerce have all been developed to the highest degree and there exists a harmonious balance between these three aspects of the economy. Here we see how protective duties – levied at the island's ports – have been a practical success. In England, with one brief interval, the productive powers of the nation have steadily increased for centuries and this has repaired the losses incurred in civil wars. Perpetual internal peace has stimulated industrial progress at home, while England's naval supremacy has prevented any decline in trade abroad. Every war that England has fought has brought about a further expansion of her foreign trade.

England holds the richest colonies in every part of the globe, while her flag dominates the seas of the world. Her trading companies and her fishermen are protected by the world's most powerful navy. And the supremacy of her navy rests upon the size and importance of England's mercantile marine and fisheries. England's powerful foreign trade is not supported by an occasional and uncertain transit trade. It rests upon the solid foundation of a gigantic industrial sector of the economy. England's manufactures are based upon highly efficient political and social institutions, upon powerful machines, upon great capital resources, upon an output larger than that of all other countries, and upon a complete network of internal transport facilities.

England has the largest capital resources in the world, and an immense manufacturing power, which can create new wealth and can be exchanged for bullion drawn from other countries. In these circumstances it seems to us that England has become the world's banker. England does not worry about her balance of trade because she never lacks commodities which can be turned into specie. One might draw an analogy between England's position in world trade and the position of the richest capitalist in a country who never needs to have a reserve of cash in hand because at any moment he can sell some of his securities and bonds.

A nation which makes goods more cheaply than anyone else and possesses immeasurably more capital than anyone else is able to grant its customers more substantial and longer credits than anyone else. In competition with its rivals such a nation will also be able to command the lion's share of the market in poorer and less advanced countries.

By accepting or by excluding the import of their raw materials and other products, England – all powerful as a manufacturing and commercial country – can confer great benefits or inflict great injuries upon nations with relatively backward economies. What England does depends upon whether her economic policy is inspired solely by self-interest and national passions and prejudices or whether her policy is inspired by a higher morality and by nobler aims. The latter is hardly to be expected at all times and in all circumstances.

All states have a common interest in defending themselves against the damage that England, enjoying world economic supremacy, can arbitrarily inflict upon their industries.

On the other hand England, with her advanced economy, could inaugurate the gradual establishment of greater freedom of trade throughout the world. But this freedom would not be achieved by insisting that states in the second and third phase of industrialisation should open their home markets to unlimited competition from English manufactured goods.

Should England pursue such a policy she would be pretending to foster the wider interests of mankind while really fostering her own selfish interests. Free competition between the advanced factories of England and the relatively backward factories of other manufacturing countries would – as we have already shown – simply lead to the destruction of the industries of the weaker states. This would mean that the countries in question would not merely give up all prospects of economic expansion in the future but would actually lose the progress that they had achieved in the past towards the establishment of a more advanced economy.

It is surely reasonable to suggest that no nation should try to hasten the future economic advance of the human race by sacrificing the progress that it has already made towards establishing its own national economic independence. Such a policy, far from being advantageous to humanity in general, would be to the sole advantage of the dominant economic nation.

Manufacturing states which have reached the second or third phase of industrialisation might hope to extend free trade by uniting with the dominant nation but such a policy should be adopted only if the special economic interests of the countries concerned are adequately safeguarded.

CHAPTER SEVEN

The Common Interest of all Manufacturing States in Free Trade

IN THIS CHAPTER we shall show that even in industrial nations there is no need – or very little need – to give tariff protection to the production of raw materials and foodstuffs, save under quite exceptional circumstances.

Moreover we have already given at any rate partial proof of the fact that many countries would be well advised to be content with a purely agrarian economy. This is desirable on the assumption that no restrictions are placed either on exporting farm products to industrial states or on importing manufactured goods from industrial states.

Experience shows that the barbarous or semi-barbarous peoples of Asia, Africa, and South America who have become civilised most quickly have always been those whom the industrialised states have provided with stable administrations, protection for persons and property, and freedom of trade. In this way backward peoples have been given the opportunity of securing manufactured goods cheaply and of selling their own products to the best advantage. Here is a great opportunity to apply the principles of the doctrine of cosmopolitan economics in a practical way. Far from injuring any country this would bring together the special interests of every nation in a valuable common enterprise.

It might, at first sight, appear to be asking too much to expect England to open her colonies to the commerce of all nations and to renounce the advantages to be gained by using her sea power to force distant backward countries – such as the states of South America – to submit to treaties which give her commercial privileges in their markets.

This is very important for the future prosperity of both advanced countries and backward and barbarous peoples. If one regards the matter from a more elevated standpoint than the sordid view taken by a merchant eager to enjoy the fruits of a monopoly, it will be seen that the introduction of the greatest possible freedom of trade would benefit not only the states in the second and third phases of industrialisation but would confer upon England greater advantages than upon anyone else.

The example of the United States shows how a country that was formerly of no importance in world trade, is able to confer great benefits upon all countries by developing her agriculture and by making great progress from an economic and social point of view. The same example illustrates the point that industrial states can promote the expansion of shipping, commerce, and manufactures much more by opening their overseas possessions to the trade of all nations than by monopolising the commerce of their colonies.

The most advanced countries in Europe and North America have the greatest possible interest in fostering the opening up and the progress of civilisation in all parts of South America, Africa, Asia and Australia. In doing so they will enormously increase their exports of manufactured goods, their imports of foreign products, their transit trade, and their shipping.

On the other hand nothing has proved to be a greater hindrance to the progress of civilisation in backward lands than the selfish and greedy policy pursued by various rival nations in different parts of the world. Advanced nations have tried to gain complete control over colonies, or exclusive influence over the administration of backward regions. Sometimes they have gained special trading rights by signing commercial treaties with the rulers of backward territories. Instead of adopting such policies, all the advanced industrial countries in the world should adopt the principle of free trade and equal rights in South America, Asia, Africa, Portugal, Spain and the Two Sicilies. A liberal policy of this kind would strike at the very root of the evil of economic selfishness. It would without doubt lead to a situation in which all industrial nations would be happy to see any one of their number undertake the task of bringing progress to barbarous peoples.

Thus England would only gain if France proclaimed a protectorate over all North Africa or if Germany embarked upon the task of promoting the progress of civilisation in Turkey and the Levant. It would be mutually beneficial to all advanced nations if their surplus populations could make use of their skills in these territories.

England's gains would be far greater than her losses because the united manufacturing power of all the industrialised countries would be far more effective than the isolated industrial power of England alone, especially if that power were hampered by the envious rivalry of other states.

It is obvious that the United States is developing into a maritime power which before long will inevitably surpass that of England. It is equally obvious that the economic interests of Canada will one day be identical with those of the United States. England would in these circumstances be well advised to give up voluntarily a supremacy that cannot in any case survive for very long. And when another nation becomes the dominant economic country in the world England will find this predominance as irksome and as unpleasant as England's dominant position is for other people today. Consequently in her own interest England should now be prepared to share her dominant position with other advanced industrial countries and should agree to the establishment of a hegemony which would secure for her advantages which would be both more substantial and longer lasting than those which she at present enjoys. Moreover new inventions – in transport and armaments – will one day deprive England of the advantages which she now enjoys because of her insular position. Then her naval and maritime power will be drastically reduced, especially if she should have to face a coalition of hostile powers. These are two very good reasons why England should now be prepared to make a commercial alliance with states in the second and third phases of industrialisation.

CHAPTER EIGHT

The Opposition of Countries to the Dominant Nation in Industry, Commerce and Sea Power

AT ALL TIMES the weaker countries in Europe have collaborated to defend themselves against the pretensions of a dominant state. This has been called the balance of power. In the same way there has been united opposition to England's dominant position with regard to industry and trade. England has become so powerful economically that she is able to bring good fortune or ill-fortune to other nations, so long as those countries act in isolation.

It is obvious that the idea of the Continental System was born because of England's excessive economic power and because of the possibility that England might misuse this power. Sooner or later the countries which have reached the second and third stage of industrialisation will have to unite to establish a new Continental System if ever England should show any inclination to use her superior sea power to injure the manufactures or commerce of these countries.

An attempt to set up a new Continental System, however, would endanger the prosperity not only of England but of all nations and –

as we have shown in the last chapter – the only satisfactory solution to the problem would be the establishment of world free trade.

Since we can hardly expect England of her own free will to make the concessions necessary to secure the establishment of a world customs union, it seems to us that the countries which have reached the second and third stage of industrialisation should form an association of their own to press for the establishment of world free trade which should be the common aim of all countries.

France and the United States should take the lead in promoting such an alliance. These two countries are closely linked by commercial ties and by their common interest in energetically furthering the maintenance of the freedom of the seas. France and the United States have similar political institutions and similar economic interests. They are natural allies and they should be prepared to take the initiative in promoting a plan which would ultimately benefit all the countries in the world.

CHAPTER NINE

The Productive Powers of Agriculture in the first Stage of Economic Development

PRIMITIVE peoples start by being hunters. Next they are engaged in pastoral activities and eventually they become arable farmers. So long as they do not trade with their neighbours the arable farmers remain in a state of virtual barbarism. This is the age of slavery, aristocracy, theocracy, and despotism. Only the great landowners are free and the wealthiest among them wield the greatest power. Tied by tyrannical laws to land which does not belong to them, the peasants are oppressed by feudal services and by the obligation to work on the estate of their lord. Their labours satisfy the needs of the landowners but they do not satisfy their own needs.

People who depend entirely upon farming and are scattered over a wide area, live in isolation and cannot meet one another. They cannot enjoy the life of a wider society. Lacking contact with each other they cannot discuss their common problems with their fellows. They are ignorant folk who have no appreciation of the arts and they do not enjoy any personal liberty. Such people cannot hope to make progress or to improve their political position so long as they are unable to set up workshops or to engage in foreign trade. The one factor which stimulates all human activities and which is the main cause of universal prosperity is missing in their lives.

Primitive peasants who simply cultivate the soil are miserable creatures, without adequate capital or tools, without culture, knowledge or any competitive spirit. Nothing encourages them to improve their situation and so they carry on with the dull routine of labour from one generation to another, happy if their crops are sufficient to pay their lord his dues. From the cradle to the grave they lead a truly wretched existence. Their physical and mental powers are never adequately used or properly developed.

These peasants appreciate neither the value of time nor the value of the land that they cultivate. Their net output – after deducting the barest necessities of life – amounts to virtually nothing. To a great extent they produce the material from which their clothes are made. Their greatest efforts produce only the most miserable results. Abstinence is their greatest achievement.

The peasant who simply tills the soil is self-sufficient and has no surplus produce to exchange for other goods. A purely arable district has no need to improve its communications with other regions. There is no stimulus to create better transport facilities which are a powerful means of improving a people's level of culture.

The failure to secure a division of labour between those who till the soil and those who make manufactured goods has another very serious drawback in as much as it leads to an undue subdivision of the land. Lacking industry to absorb the surplus population the growth of a population entirely dependent upon the soil must lead to a continual reduction in the size of the farms and smallholdings. Peasants themselves consume nearly everything that they produce and are able to save only a small surplus to keep in reserve.

For this reason – and because of inadequate means of transport – a failure of the harvest leads to famine and epidemics. The standard of farming is so poor – the lack of scientific management is so obvious – that no surplus is produced that could be used for commerce or for industry. The primitive peasant is able to consume very few products of industry and sometimes he cannot consume any at all. He has no surplus to devote to the education of his children, to his own enjoyment, or to his intellectual advancement.

In these circumstances good harvests and an increase in the population have the great disadvantage that they provide the rulers of such regions with the means to engage in needless wars with the result that the wretched standard of life of the peoples sinks to a position of utter misery and degradation.

The intellectual powers of such a people are hardly awakened and are put to little use. There are no opportunities for latent talents to be developed. Only physical exertion secures rewards and they are poor enough since the landowners monopolise the labour of the workers on their land.

Such people have few contacts with each other or with neighbouring peoples. The activities of the individual are confined to a single village. In these circumstances inefficiency, prejudices, bad habits, and vices survive for centuries. Physical strength is the dominant factor in such societies. Moral strength never makes its mark and never triumphs over brute force.

CHAPTER TEN

The Productive Powers of Agriculture in the second Stage of Economic Development

WHEN FOREIGN trade brings manufactured goods into a country in exchange for agricultural products a dramatic change occurs in the agrarian economy. Farmers are able to obtain better machines and tools which are more efficient for the tasks that they have to perform. They are followed by new processes and improvements of every kind, such as new crops and better and more useful stock. From abroad come new ideas and new capital. An injection of cash into the economy enables those who work on the land to make many desirable improvements. In such a situation new needs are created and an improved standard of life appears to be possible. This in turn stimulates new economic activities and promotes a new spirit of enterprise. The productive powers of agriculture are fostered in a thousand different ways.

Foreign trade fosters the export of certain agricultural products such as wool, hemp, wine and cereals. It also stimulates the division of labour among those working on the land and it encourages them to specialise in growing particular crops. Those who, thanks to the nature of their soil and to climatic conditions, are able to produce foodstuffs for export will concentrate their activities on one particular branch of agriculture. On the other hand they will start to buy those (farm) products which their neighbours can produce more cheaply. The demand from abroad for their products, the new division of labour, and the development of an exchange of (farm) products within the agricultural community will enable all who work on the land to increase their output. At the same time internal commerce will steadily expand.

In time agricultural products themselves take on the character of exchangeable goods. People with money to spare will realise the advantage of purchasing farm produce when it is cheap and of storing it until prices rise after a poor harvest or because of an increased demand from abroad. Society is better off and famines will become a thing of the past, as prices become stable and the net output of agriculture increases. With the growth of agricultural revenues the price of land rises while credit is more readily available. The incomes of tenant farmers, the rents collected by landowners, and the wages of labourers all rise. Since landowners and tenants both desire to secure the maximum output from the land, they will co-operate to sink new capital into agriculture and to improve methods of farming.

At the same time people will begin to recognise how feudal rights impose restrictions upon production and upon internal trade. They will see the drawbacks of feudalism and they will appreciate the need for sound laws and institutions which will guarantee the liberty of the individual, the security of workers, the safety of property, and the progress of education and culture. As internal and external commerce expands people will appreciate the advantages of improved transport facilities.

This is a time when farmers, manufacturers, and merchants unite to support free trade. It is the golden age of the motto: "Laissez faire et lassez passer".

In this period a nation's industries begin to develop. As people see the prospect of enjoying a better standard of living there is a strong demand for manufactured products. Some of these may not be available from foreign countries. Others may be made more cheaply at home than abroad because of the country's resources, the existence of a low level of wages, or other circumstances. At first when industry is stimulated by foreign commerce, manufacturers join with farmers in supporting free trade which is advantageous to both. But as native industries grow so manufacturers realise that their progress is being restricted by the import of foreign goods. At the same time those who work on the land come to appreciate the fact that the home market is much larger, more stable, more certain, and more profitable than foreign markets.

It is dangerous to allow the prosperity of a country's arable land to be entirely dependent upon the export of cereals and raw materials in exchange for manufactured products. Such agricultural exports are liable to serious fluctuations. The amount of produce purchased annually by the importing countries depends upon the size of their own harvests. When they have to import foodstuffs they seek to buy in the cheapest market. From time to time it may be to their advantage to purchase their requirements from a new source of supply. In such circumstances an agricultural country may find that it has no market for its surplus produce.

Moreover every year an agrarian country draws advance payments from an industrial country in respect of sales of foodstuffs and raw materials and it has generally spent the proceeds of its future sales even before the crops have been harvested. A crisis, affecting merchants and farmers alike, will occur if there is a poor harvest or if the orders from the industrial country are insufficient to cover the advance payments. Agriculturalists seek a more regular and a more reliable market for their products at home to avoid these crises and the uncertainty of foreign orders. Unfortunately, owing to foreign competition, native industries have, at this stage, not developed sufficiently to guarantee the farmers a secure market for their produce at home. Indeed centuries may pass before native manufacturers become strong enough to do so unless, of course, a war or a decline in the output of the industrial countries gives them the opportunity to expand.

Wars between nations break the bonds of commerce that link agricultural and industrial countries. During hostilities farmers and smallholders can no longer sell their raw materials and foodstuffs to an industrialised country. Similarly manufacturers in an industrialised country lose their market in an agricultural country in time of war. It is for these reasons that nations come to be thrown on their own resources to satisfy their needs. And this is the crucial moment when the industrialists in an agricultural country, who have long struggled against foreign competition begin to wake up.

At first industrialists will not be able to supply the rural community with manufactured goods which are as cheap or as good as those supplied by foreigners. But in time, by improving methods of production, they will be able to do so. The industrialists will not at first be able to compensate the rural community for all the losses sustained by the interruption of its contacts with foreign markets. The rural community will not buy from native industrialists as many manufactured goods as it formerly purchased from abroad and it will have to pay higher prices for home produced goods of poorer quality. So those who work on the land will suffer a double loss.

In time, however, the situation will change. Stimulated by wartime conditions and by the new profits which they are making, the native manufacturers will begin to compete among themselves. When this happens the rural community will appreciate that it has on its own doorstep new home industries which will one day be far more useful to it than the foreign manufacturers with whom they formerly dealt. Those who work on the land will realise that they now secure manufactured goods from a stable source and that these products will be available in wartime as well as in peace time.

In the event of a long war the progress made by native manufacturers will be such that the agrarian community will see that tariff protection for industry against foreign competition will be in its own interest. As soon as hostilities cease the merchants engaged in foreign trade will certainly press for the return of a free exchange of goods between the former belligerents. Once more their motto – once echoed throughout the land – will be: Laissez faire, laissez passer.

On the other hand the industrialists will now demand the exclusion of foreign manufactured goods so that they can continue to enjoy the monopoly of the home market that was theirs during the war. They will argue that since they are not yet strong enough to stand on their own feet, they could be ruined if free trade were established between the two countries as it was before the war. Free trade would soon reduce native industry to its former impotent position and all the sacrifices made by farmers and manufacturers during the war would be lost. If hostilities were renewed the country would have to make the same sacrifices all over again. Manufacturers argue that a prohibitive tariff giving them protection similar to what they enjoyed during the war would enable them in time to become powerful enough to withstand foreign competition. They point to the advantages that those who work on the land will eventually secure through their contacts with a fully developed home industry, which can never be destroyed by any future war and which will consequently grow from strength to strength.

The agrarian sector of the economy has to decide upon what attitude it should, in its own interest, adopt with regard to the claims of merchants engaged in foreign commerce and of industrialists engaged in producing manufactured goods at home. Those who work on the land hold the balance of power between these rival claims. Whichever side it supports will be the victor. Agriculturalists are in a position to choose between apparent immediate short term advantages and ultimate real long term advantages. Free trade offers the agriculturalists the apparent immediate advantage of securing higher prices for their exports and of paying lower prices for the manufactured goods that they import from abroad. On the other hand protection offers them for the future all the advantages that they have been offered by the native manufacturers. If those who work on the land are capable of grasping the full implications of the situation they will show true patriotism and they will support a protectionist policy which will lay the foundations of the future prosperity and greatness of the nation.

Free trade is the fantasy of the merchants engaged in foreign commerce and if it wins the day, most of the home industries that have developed during the war will collapse and the workers they employ will have to find new jobs on the land.

The collapse of the industries of a predominantly agrarian country would substantially reduce the demand for farm products and would also lead to an expansion of the work force on the land. This would bring about the overproduction of agricultural produce and would also lead to a fall in the price of such produce. The surplus produce which is not absorbed by the home market will be exported to an industrial country, with the result that in this country too the price of farm products will fall.

Thus what happens to the agrarian sector of the economy in a predominantly agrarian country affects the state of agriculture in an industrialised country. Just as industry develops rapidly in wartime in an agricultural country so there will be an expansion of agriculture in an industrialised state. In wartime the inability to import farm products causes prices of such products to rise and substantial capital has to be invested in agriculture in an industrialised state to increase output on existing cultivated land and to bring new land under the plough.

An expansion in the demand for agricultural products causes prices to rise. Rents, profits, and wages also go up and there is an increase in the labour force on the land and in the output of farm produce. After the war agricultural products from abroad – such as large quantities of cheap grain – come onto the market once more. The industrialised country is now faced with an agricultural crisis similar to the industrial crisis that afflicted the agricultural country. And the farmers in the industrial country will demand the imposition of high import duties to keep out the farm products of the agricultural country.

If the complaints of the agricultural classes in an industrialised country are ignored, the situation in both states – the agrarian and the industrialised country – will gradually return to what it was before the war. Should hostilities be resumed everything will again be turned upside down and the events of the first war will simply be repeated. But if the farmers in the industrialised country are protected by a tariff against competition from the agrarian country, a different kind of war will break out – a tariff war of import duties.

Should the agricultural products of an agrarian country be denied access to the markets of an industrialised state, the farmers in the agrarian country will suffer severely. They will realise that they are gaining no advantage from buying cheap manufactured goods from an industrialised country if they cannot pay for these goods by exporting their farm produce. Then they will remember the benefits that they received in the days when the industries of their country were flourishing. Then they will realise that they have gained nothing by sacrificing their country's factories. Then they will see the permanent prosperity of agriculture must be based upon the existence of a strong national industry. And now they too will demand tariffs so that the industry of their country may be protected from all threats from abroad and may expand. In the historical part of our treatise we will show how natural is this development. Here we will simply observe that we have demonstrated how prohibitions and protective tariffs are the natural consequences of national rivalries and wars. They are not the invention of some doctrinaire economist.

CHAPTER ELEVEN

The Productive Powers of Agriculture in the third Stage of Economic Development

IN THE LAST chapter we showed

1. That in an agrarian country agriculture can become important only in association with the industry of that country.

2. That in an agrarian country agriculture is raised from the first to the second stage of development through foreign trade – which is simply co-operation between the farmers of an agrarian country and the industrialists of an industrialised country.

3. That this co-operation may be interrupted or may come to an end altogether if hostilities break out between the agrarian country and the industrialised country.

4. That certain consequences follow from the ending of this co-operation:

   (a) The farmers in the agrarian state try to promote the industrial development of their own country

   (b) The industrialised country attempts to foster the development of agriculture.

5. That these factors inevitably lead to international rivalry and to the imposition of tariffs and prohibitions.

In this chapter we propose to explain how the agriculture of a country can flourish, can expand, can gain security for the future, and can be protected against every relapse and every crisis. To achieve this state of affairs it is necessary that agriculture and industry should be physically close together and that their close co-operation should not be interrupted by natural causes or by any political action. Moreover all branches of the country's industry must be fully developed and there must be a harmonious balance between production and consumption and between the two main groups in the population – those who work on the land and those who are engaged in industry.

The third stage in the development of agriculture begins when the industries of the nation dominate the whole – or nearly the whole – of the home market. This dominance may have been secured either by the inherent strength of the industries concerned or by the protection afforded by a tariff.

In the first and second stages of development the agriculture of an agrarian country is dependent upon the industries of a foreign country. Agriculture enjoys the following advantages when it reaches the third stage of development:

1. When manufactures are fully developed, agriculture can usually sell products at a higher price than before in the industrial home market and buy its manufactured goods at a lower price than would be possible if an exchange of products took place between the agrarian country and a foreign industrialised state . The closer the farms are situated to the factories, the lower are the costs charged by merchants and carriers for effecting the exchange of agricultural products and manufactured goods. The time and capital needed to bring about the exchange are reduced. And the exchange will not be hampered by natural causes, by wars, or by commercial crises. The exchange can take place with great regularity and is protected against fluctuations of trade. Indeed the more harmonious the co-operation between producers and consumers the fewer are the slumps that hinder the exchange of goods.[1]

1. Chaptal (*De l'industrie françoise*, Part II, p. 203) estimates that in 1819 the value of the output of industrial goods was 1,820 million francs. He estimates the profits of manufacturers at only 182 million francs. The rest includes the cost of raw materials, wages, etc. French industry (excluding the consumption of the industrialists) provided French agriculture with a market for its produce valued at 1,638 million francs.

2. Thousands of products in the possession of landowners which were formerly of little or no value now increase greatly in value. These include waterfalls, building materials, sand, stones, chalk, gypsum, and all kinds of soil and materials. In addition there is land suitable for the workshops, dwellings, and gardens of the manufacturers.

3. A new demand will be created for many products for which formerly there was little if any demand – cattle for fattening, meat, poultry, eggs, butter, cheese, fruit, vegetables, straw, hay, and oats for horses – which the manufacturers need for work or pleasure. There will be demand for tobacco and for plants producing oils and dyestuffs. By purchasing these products, most of which are best produced by smallholders, the industrialists give those who work on the land the opportunity to improve their condition and to make more money.

4. Nothing is more important for industrialists than the availability of cheap fuel and also easy, speedy, and regular transport at a low cost for all the products and raw materials which they need to build factories and to produce manufactured goods. Consequently industrialists hasten to promote the expansion of communications within a country. They foster the construction of highways, canals, and railways and the improvement of navigable rivers. Moreover they turn these improvements into lucrative industrial undertakings. In countries with deposits of coal and peat the existence of improved transport facilities will enable landowners to draw the fuel they need from distant regions. Areas which, lacking such fuel, would be planted with trees can be used to raise much more profitable crops. And there will be an increased demand for farm produce on the part of those who work in the mines.

5. The demand for a variety of farm products (paragraph 3 above) and the improvement of communications (paragraph 4 above) are factors which greatly stimulate specialisation on the land. Indeed, this process has already begun in the second stage of agricultural production. Hilly districts concentrate entirely upon forestry, mining, cattle, and sheep and draw their foodstuffs from arable districts which are better suited to growing cereals. In the plains cattle can be fattened for the market. In short every region can specialise in the agricultural production for which it is favoured by nature. In return each region draws from other parts of the country those products which are not grown or raised locally. This

division of labour – or rather division of products – will greatly increase the output of agriculture.

6. As it expands industry will accumulate capital of its own and will also attract new capital from abroad. Money from these sources which may not be needed to improve or to extend existing factories can frequently be made available to agriculture. Loans can be made to landowners for agricultural improvements. Alternatively industrialists themselves can invest money in landed property which they can improve. This will lead to an increase in the price of land. The productive powers of the land will expand and will be advantageous to the whole agricultural sector of the economy.

7. As industry develops in a country so the subdivision of farm land into smallholdings will cease. There will be a more rational division of the land. We condemn as harmful the division of farm land into numerous tiny smallholdings because their owners can hope to attain only a very low standard of living. A large farmer or landowner, on the other hand, is his own manufacturer, his own producer, his own consumer, and his own wage earner. Since home industry stimulates a large demand for farm products and a demand for labour, the existence of a surplus output from the farms no longer promotes the undue subdivision of agricultural land. On the contrary it helps to feed the factory workers and it promotes an increase in the number of industrial workers. Large estates will become common because they can produce the surplus agricultural produce which industry needs. The demand for farm products that we have mentioned in paragraph 3 (above) promotes a very useful specialisation in agriculture. Some farmers raise fat cattle; others make dairy products. Some grow vegetables, others have orchards. In addition there are allotments in the towns which the factory workers cultivate as a recreation.

8. If a region becomes industrialised the local smallholders, farm workers and their families have an opportunity of making good use of time which was formerly wasted, particularly during the winter months. Now the factories will be able to provide them with useful employment. This applies particularly to women, old people, children, cripples, and the infirm. The labour of these people is of little use on the land but can be most useful in industry.

9. The development of manufactures demands a great many skills and those who possess such skills have the opportunity of using their abilities in various branches of manufacture. Skilled

workers earn enough to live in comfort and some may even become rich. Agriculture benefits from the growth of industry because children growing up on the land who have mechanical aptitudes can be trained for an industrial occupation. If no industry existed – and therefore no jobs for skilled workers – these children would have to choose between emigrating and facing a dull life on the land.

10. In general it appears that agriculture shares with industry in all the advantages brought about by the growth of manufactures. These advantages include not only the development of political freedom, but advances in learning, the arts, literature, and education. There are also improvements in public institutions, in national defence, and in taxation. It is obvious that two people have a better chance of defending themselves than one individual has of defending himself alone. Similarly two people can carry a greater burden of taxation than one person. This is still more obvious when a person who owns nothing except his physical strength as his means of subsistence, is supported by a person whose knowledge and skill is united with the power of machinery.

11. It can be shown that in favourable circumstances a farmer and his family can produce enough provisions to feed an industrial worker and his family. Similarly a factory worker can provide someone who lives in the country with the tools and other manufactured products that he requires. Taking account only of the internal production and the internal consumption of a country, a balance is struck between the agricultural and the industrial populations when the two are equal in numbers. French industry will be fully developed when the 20 million persons working on the land can feed and keep employed 20 million workers in industry. In prosperous times those working in industry will consume foodstuffs and raw materials to the value of at least 150 to 200 francs a head. French industry would then buy French farm produce to the value of 3 to 4 milliard francs. This is certainly more than France could ever hope to sell abroad if it were to remain a purely agrarian country. It follows that once home industries are fully developed, those who make a living on the land have obtained a far larger and more valuable market than they could find in the whole world, however free international trade might be.

12. The advantages which the agrarian sector of the community secures in the home market when industry is fully developed are shared by certain specialised branches of agriculture, which are

suited to a particular country. The vineyards of France may serve as an example. A comparison between the output and the export of wine shows that France consumes ten times as much wine as it sends abroad. It is clear that the ability to send their wines freely all over the world would not compensate the vineyard owners for the consequent loss to the nation's manufacturing powers at home.[1]

13. When a nation has succeeded in fully developing both agriculture and industry and in securing a satisfactory balance between them, the consumption of each of these sectors of the economy will exactly equal the production of the other.

In this situation a country can look forward for centuries to come to the continued expansion of its productive powers, wealth, national strength, economic prosperity, and cultural progress. On the other hand a nation which depends upon foreigners for its manufactured goods is liable to experience all the disturbances and crises which we mentioned in the previous chapter.

It is this reciprocal activity between the two sectors of the economy – the agrarian and the industrial – which explains both the extent and the strength of England's productive powers. And this reciprocal activity has not been interrupted during centuries of steady progress.

These factors taken together influence the revenues, the value and the price of all landed property in the country. There is no better measure of the prosperity of a nation than the price of landed property. Every advance in agriculture or industry is reflected in an increase in the price of urban and rural land. Every decline in

---

1. [List's note] Chaptal estimates the total value of the production of French wines and spirits at 718 million francs (*De l'industrie françoise*, Part I, p. 177). He estimates the value of the exports in the period 1786-90 (when it had without doubt reached its peak) at 51 million francs. So the value of the wine consumed at home is 14 times as great as the value of the wine exported. Chaptal estimates that the consumption of wine in France amounts to 22 francs per head. So 2,200,000 Frenchmen consume as much wine as was exported when exports were at their peak. Since it is well known that the industrial population consumes on average more wine per head than the agrarian population the above figure may be reduced to 1,500,000. Today the industrial population of France is 10,000,000. One can hardly doubt that with the expansion of agriculture and industry the populations of the two sectors will one day be equal. In other words the industrial population of France will be 20,000,000 at some time in the future. These 20,000,000 will then drink from six to eight times as much wine in a year as France has ever exported. This shows how important the expansion of French industry will be for the French vine growers and how little substance there is in their assertion that they will be ruined by tariffs imposed to protect manufacturers.

agriculture or industry is reflected in a fall in the price of land. Everywhere the price of property is high or low according to the strength or weakness of the productive powers of the nation. It can be shown that a nation which invests 100 million francs in new factories increases the value of its landed property by five to ten times that amount. And the author of this treatise will certainly submit statistical proof of this assertion. This factor in the situation is of great significance when it is necessary to find out whether the creation of a national industry by means of import duties can be achieved in some way other than at the expense of the consumers – that is to say those whose livelihood depends upon the land.[1]

A fourth stage in the development of agriculture remains to be considered but we do this only after we have examined the leading characteristics of manufacturing industry.

CHAPTER TWELVE

The Productive Powers of Industry

INDUSTRY is the mother and father of science, literature, the arts, enlightenment, freedom, useful institutions, and national power and independence.

Anyone who wishes to devote himself to industrial activity – to

1. [List's note] Chaptal (*De l'industrie françoise,* Part I, p. 225) estimates at 37,522 million francs the total value of the capital of property and agricultural land in France. It is certain that industry has played an important part in creating this capital. The value of landed property is ten times higher in England than in Poland. If we assume that French industry – as yet not fully developed – has already been responsible for a five fold increase in the value of French landed property then this increase in wealth, which benefits only the landowners, may be estimated at 30,000 million francs. When French industry is fully developed this figure will be doubled. The expansion in agricultural wealth is equivalent to 170 times the total annual profits of manufacturers. This proves that industrialists do not become rich at the expense of those who make a living from the land. In fact those who work in the industrial and the agrarian sectors of the economy make each other rich.

the production of manufactured goods – should learn and understand something of mathematics and the natural sciences. Schoolmasters and books are needed to enable those engaged in industrial pursuits to make progress in these subjects. They are needed to give young people possessing the appropriate natural ability and previous education the opportunity to specialise in mathematics and the natural sciences.

As a nation becomes more industrialised it becomes more necessary to secure the services of suitable trained people in the factories and workshops. Such people are now able to command higher salaries and wages than was formerly possible. It will be easier for them to devote themselves entirely to a particular branch of knowledge, provided that they have the necessary natural aptitude and a good preliminary training. Knowledge is becoming more specialised. It is clear that all branches of knowledge – particularly those which can be applied to industrial pursuits – are making rapid progress.

The greater the advance in scientific knowledge, the more numerous will be the new inventions which save labour and raw materials and lead to the discovery of new products and processes. As those engaged in industry become more familiar with the advances made in scientific knowledge the more quickly – and the more successfully – will new discoveries and inventions be applied to industry in a practical way.

Anyone engaged in industrial pursuits should appreciate that success will depend upon his knowledge of science and upon the new discoveries that are the result of scientific progress. If he does not already possess certain qualities he should develop the art of independent thought and the ability to make decisions. A man acquires intellectual qualities and imagination not only from schoolmasters and books but by travelling and by associating with those who have ambitions similar to his own. He should be in touch not only with men who are in the same line of business as himself but he should also associate with those engaged in various other aspects of the world of business and also with men who devote their talents to public affairs. A man with this sort of training and experience will soon realise that if he is to succeed in business and gain a fair reward for his work he will need as firm guarantees as possible for his personal safety and for the security of his property. His experiences of life – and an appreciation of the nature of his own interests –

should lead him to support the abolition of anything that restricts his freedom and the prosperity of his enterprises. He should support the establishment of national institutions that will ensure his freedom and increase his prosperity.

In countries where arable farming has been practised for centuries it is rare to find men who rise from poverty to enjoy first a modest competence and then wealth and complete financial independence. Industry, on the other hand, offers men who start at the bottom the chance of rising to the very top by using their abilities and by working hard. The possibility of such an achievement provides a stimulus for the whole working population.

A country devoted entirely to agriculture esteems really sturdy physical strength most highly and accords it the greatest financial rewards. In such a society the whole range of intellectual and moral powers is virtually non-existent. But industry calls forth and promotes the growth of intellectual and moral forces of every kind.[1]

In the previous chapter we have shown how the productive powers of industry awaken in industry and agriculture the spirit of enterprise and innovation. We have seen how a great many natural resources – formerly of little or no value – have become increasingly valuable as industry expands. We have explained that industry promotes the division of labour in agriculture, increases the demand for new farm products, stimulates the improvement of communications, and checks the harmful subdivision of land into tiny smallholdings, while fostering a sensible division of landed property. We have shown how industry gives scope for the expansion of all kinds of skills and abilities as well as increasing the revenues and value of land. We have made it clear that normally agriculture can prosper only insofar as industry also prospers and becomes more efficient.

Agriculture gives little scope for the abilities of skilled and useful workers. Factories, on the other hand, do give them the opportunity to use their skill so that their productive powers are multiplied by 10 or even by 100. Consequently an industrialised society will gain immeasurably more from new inventions and from scientific progress than is possible for an agrarian society.

A division of labour can be usefully developed in agriculture only insofar as it is brought about and stimulated by differences of soil

1. [List's note] Charles Dupin, *Forces prod.*, p. 92. [The full reference is Charles Dupin, *Forces productives et commerciales de la France* (two volumes, Paris, 1827), Vol. I, pp. 89-92.]

and climate. On the other hand the various branches of industry can give unlimited scope for the division of labour. The productive powers of agriculture are scattered over a wide area. But the productive powers of industry are brought together and are centralised at one place. This process of concentration eventually creates an expansion of productive powers which grow in geometric rather than in arithmetic proportion.

This is why the population of an industrialised society is brought together in a few conurbations in which are concentrated a great variety of technical skills, productive powers, applied science, art and literature. Here are to be found great public and private institutions and associations in which theoretical knowledge is applied to the practical affairs of industry and commerce. Only in such conurbations can a public opinion develop which is strong enough to vanquish mere brute force, to maintain freedom for all, and to insist that the public authorities should adopt administrative policies that will promote and safeguard national prosperity.

Just as the towns draw their foodstuffs from farms scattered over a wide area, so the farms secure from the towns the means to improve their living standards, to stimulate their intellectual needs, and to meet their need to improve their social and political conditions.

In addition the manufacturers are the focus of a large, lucrative, and world wide trade with peoples of varied standards of culture who live in many distant countries. Industry turns cheap bulky raw materials, which cannot be sent long distances, into goods of low weight and high value which are in universal demand.

The market for agricultural products is limited by their weight, by their low value in relation to their weight, and by the availability of transport facilities. Moreover primitive and semi-civilised societies usually produce all the foodstuffs and raw materials that they need – with some to spare – but they do not manufacture industrial goods.

A country with a predominantly agrarian economy cannot trade with primitive societies – and most societies in the world fall into this category. Primitive peoples already possess everything that a predominantly agrarian economy has to offer and they do not produce anything that a predominantly agrarian economy requires.

But the manufacturers in an industrialised country can acquire sufficient gold and silver to finance the steady expansion of its international trade and to curb fluctuations in prices. Only an industrialised country can establish colonies and link them to the mother country by a mutually profitable exchange of goods.

We have shown that it is factories that make possible the establishment of a substantial and permanent foreign trade. Consequently the prosperity of the mercantile marine is also based upon growing industries. Transit trade alone can never be a satisfactory basis for the development of shipping and we shall illustrate this from the example of the Hansa Towns (chapter 29).

In the previous chapter we explained that a country can double and treble its population and output by monopolising the home market through its national productive powers. The financial and military strength of the nation grows in the same proportion.

We think that we have now made it clear that if a country desires to ensure its national independence and to achieve a high degree of prosperity, wealth, and power, it must possess highly developed and efficient industries.

CHAPTER THIRTEEN

The Productive Powers of Industry (continued)

THE COSMOPOLITAN THEORISTS do not question the importance of industrial expansion. They assume, however, that this can be achieved by adopting the policy of free trade and by leaving individuals to pursue their own private interests. They believe that in such circumstances a country will automatically secure the development of those branches of manufacture which are best suited to its own particular situation. They consider that government action to stimulate the establishment of industries does more harm than good.

In our first chapter we observed that the situation existing in a world of universal peace – as is assumed by the dominant school of economics – bears no relation to the situation that actually exists in a world of national rivalries and wars. In our second chapter we showed how in the real world the countries with the most advanced economies are forced to promote the development of those branches of manufacture that are suited to their particular needs. And such countries would have to do this if only to secure the growth and the prosperity of their agriculture. Finally in our last chapter we have submitted evidence proving that an efficient and highly developed industry is essential if a country is to expand its revenues, wealth, and armaments and if it is to make progress in the arts of civilisation. In this chapter we propose to show that countries in the second or third phase of industrialisation also need protective tariffs in order to challenge the economic power of the dominant industrial state. The very nature of their industries makes it essential for them to adopt such a fiscal policy.

A national industry in which all branches of manufacture are highly developed is a plant of slow growth. Many generations may pass before a people can achieve such a high standard of industry, especially if social or political obstacles delay the development of the economy. National industry can expand only insofar as progress also occurs in education, culture, and political freedom. The removal of obstacles brought about by faulty institutions or laws is also necessary. Moreover the agrarian sector of the economy must be able to supply industry with the raw materials, the foodstuffs, and the market for manufactured goods that it requires.

Even when all these conditions have been met, a long time will have to be allowed for training the necessary number of civil engineers, industrial chemists, mechanics, and factory managers. And still more time will be needed to turn people accustomed to working on the land into keen skilled factory workers. Only traditions passed on from one generation to another can imbue men with a genuine preference for a particular industrial occupation – the sort of dedication that even makes a miner prefer life underground to life behind the plough.

It takes a long time for both factory managers and factory workers to learn step by step how to perfect machines, tools, and manufacturing processes. Only after a long series of experiments is it possible for the manager of a factory to turn out a perfect product.

Not only the quality but also the price of the goods produced in a factory must be satisfactory. The price of goods is determined by the level of wages paid in the factory, by the interest payable on the capital invested in the factory, and by the quantity of goods produced.

The work of the less skilled men in the factory is not only the most expensive but also the worst. Some men have a natural aptitude for farm work and they follow this occupation by inclination. To persuade them to turn to a new industrial occupation, the factory manager must make the work attractive by offering higher wages than those earned in agriculture. The wages of labour are determined by supply and demand and when a new factory is established the relationship between supply and demand – as far as labour is concerned – is distorted in a manner unfavourable to the factory owner.

In predominantly agricultural countries investors are accustomed to demand solid guarantees before they invest their money. Since the erection of a new factory is always a hazardous enterprise it is not surprising that capitalists often hesitate to support such an undertaking. If they do invest in a new factory they will demand a bonus in the shape of higher interest. In these circumstances a factory owner has to pay heavily for the capital that he borrows to found his enterprise.

A factory owner also needs cheap raw materials and fuel. Even if they are available in adequate quantities in the country in which the factory is situated, their cost will depend upon the efficiency of the transport system. In a predominantly agricultural country, communications are generally very poor. The result is a vicious circle. Efficient highways and canals produce no revenues. The need for a good transport system is not felt until large industries have developed. Yet large industries cannot grow in a country until adequate communications have been provided.

The cheapest and best methods of obtaining the necessary raw materials and of marketing the finished manufactured goods are discovered only by a process of trial and error lasting many years. At first sales may be poor, or at least uncertain. But the greater the uncertainty and the smaller the sales the higher are the prices that the factory owner must charge for his goods.

Regarded as isolated enterprises there are grave drawbacks that newly established factories have to overcome.

It is also obvious that the success of one branch of industry always depends upon the success of another branch of industry. An iron-master who makes pig iron cannot make a profit if he is unable to secure supplies of cheap fuel because the local collieries have not been sufficiently developed. Nor can he make a profit unless there are in existence enough foundries, steelworks, and engineering plants to buy the pig iron that he produces.

Every factory needs to operate in association with countless other enterprises which supply raw materials, buy the finished product, or construct and maintain machinery. No factory reaches its maximum efficiency unless all the factories with which it is linked have also reached their maximum efficiency.

We believe that we have now shown what difficulties have to be overcome by all new manufacturing enterprises. We have shown that all factories are linked together and that one cannot succeed unless the others also succeed. And we have explained why it takes such a long time for a factory to reach its full potential and maximum efficiency.

We will now compare and contrast the manufacturing power of states in the second and third phases of industrialisation with the economy of the dominant industrial state. We will compare countries which are still moving towards full industrialisation with those which have successfully completed the process of industrialisation.

A fully industrialised state is one which has successfully completed the process of industrialisation and has managed to overcome all the obstacles which we have already discussed. Such a state has numerous trained engineers, mechanics, industrial chemists, and factory workers whose skills are based upon technical knowledge and practical experience. Sufficient skilled workers are available at modest wages. The most efficient tools and machines are being used in modern factory buildings. The original capital borrowed to launch the enterprise has long been repaid. The undertaking now enjoys the confidence of investors. The factory owner can now borrow money that he needs at a reasonable rate of interest. Local communications have reached a high level of efficiency. All branches of industry have expanded in an orderly fashion. Manufacturers are now assured of regular supplies of raw materials and of markets in which to sell their goods. In these circumstances there is a high output of goods of the best quality which are being offered for sale at the lowest possible price.

If, under conditions of free trade, a struggle should take place between countries at different stages of economic development it is inevitable that the most backward country would go to the wall. And what would be the consequence of the collapse of industry in a relatively backward country?

Manufacturers who had acquired the necessary knowledge and experience would settle in foreign countries. Workers would have to learn a new trade, change their jobs, emigrate, or sink into a condition of miserable poverty. Nearly all the capital invested in factory buildings, tools and machinery would be lost. The confidence of investors in industrial enterprises would vanish if not for ever at any rate for a long time. There would be a dramatic decline in the traffic on the roads, rivers, and canals. The output of mines would also decline. All progress would come to an end. There would be a steady decline in the public revenues, in the power of the nation, in the rents collected by landowners, and in the value of landed property. In fact the country would relapse into a state of barbarism from which it could be rescued only by reversing the process of decline by again stimulating industrial progress by means of tariff protection. Such a policy would eventually enable a country to resume its former position among the states of the world as an independent civilised nation.

In an age of great inventions, such as the one in which we are now living, it is impossible to assess the influence of new technical discoveries either upon particular branches of manufacture or upon industry as a whole which are at present in the second or third phase of industrial development. In fact the manufacturers of the dominant manufacturing country who sell their products in extensive markets all over the world will feel the urge to exploit the invention as quickly as possible and to snatch it from under the noses of the manufacturers of the relatively backward industrial countries so as to produce goods even more cheaply than before. This would enable them to widen their market and to make bigger profits. The expenses incurred through being the first in the field would be more than covered by additional profits earned later. The capital at their disposal and their ability to raise loans would make it possible for them to make financial sacrifices so as to be able to exploit a new invention. On the other hand the manufacturers in a relatively backward industrial country would still be paying off their initial capital and would not be able to raise additional capital either by using their own resources or by borrowing in the open market. Consequently they would not be in a position to exploit the invention. In this way it could happen that a large part of the industry of a less advanced nation might collapse simply because a more advanced state was able to exploit a new invention a few years before a weaker rival could do so.

Moreover it should be appreciated that the balance between supply and demand is generally upset at regular intervals – five to ten years – and this causes commercial crises. During a slump the free exchange of goods between factories in different countries is replaced by a war to the death. Inevitably the firms which go under are those which have the lowest cash reserves and are least able to pay interest on their loans. They are the firms which are not able to grant credit to their customers. They cannot earn a sufficient profit to cover their immediate expenses and they cannot survive trading losses. These firms cannot keep their factories going and they cannot survive unscathed until the coming of better times.

Finally, as we mentioned in the previous chapter, it is necessary to appreciate the significance of national industrial power in time of war.

For a state in the second or third phase of industrialisation there can be no doubt that it is both necessary and desirable to adopt the fiscal policy of protection.

The protection which a nation can give to its industries will be more effective if certain conditions are fulfilled:

1. The policy of protection should be in accord with the natural and human resources – as well as the social and political structure – of the nation.
2. The policy should aid not only manufacturers but also mining and agriculture.
3. The policy should ensure a steady expansion of industrial output.
4. The policy should safeguard industry and agriculture from fluctuations in trade and from slumps.
5. The policy should stimulate the competitive power of a country's industries. In time these industries should be able to face foreign competition successfully. The policy of protection should, however, continue to ensure the further expansion of the country's industries.
6. The policy of protection should be adjusted so that foreign capital and skill are attracted to a country.

7. The policy of protection should be so well balanced and should be established on so firm a basis that it cannot be harmed by any measures – legal or otherwise – taken (by foreigners) to oppose it.

————————

CHAPTER FOURTEEN

Does the Development of Industry withdraw Capital from Agriculture?

THE COSMOPOLITAN THEORISTS do not deny that prohibitions and import duties can bring into existence what they call "artificial" industries. But they do deny that this is to the advantage of a country. They regard such "artificial" industries as hot house plants that attract capital away from more useful economic activities, which would foster the expansion of the national economy (for example in agriculture) in a natural manner.

In all abstract branches of knowledge there is a serious misuse of technical terms which are not strictly defined. Thus in economics the word "capital" is particularly liable to misuse.[1] Economic theorists apply the word to all sorts of quite different things such as

1. [List's note] Readers of the last 6 and the next 6 chapters of my treatise will know how to judge correctly the following argument of Adam Smith (Vol. II, p. 179):

> That this monopoly of the home market frequently gives great encouragement to that particular species of industry which enjoys it, and frequently turns towards that employment a greater share of both the labour and stock of the society than would otherwise have gone to it, cannot be doubted. But whether it tends either to increase the general industry of the society, or to give it the most advantageous direction, is not perhaps altogether so evident ...
> The general industry of the society can never exceed what the capital of the society can employ. As the number of workmen that can be kept in employment by any particular person must bear a certain proportion to his capital, so the number of those that can be continually employed by all the members of a great

money, machinery, labour, population, or the intellectual qualities of a people. The word has been applied to the natural resources which men can use. But to check the validity of the conclusions drawn by economists it is necessary to know exactly what they mean when they use the word "capital".

In order to refute the objection to which we have referred above it is necessary that we should examine the various ways in which the word "capital" has been used by supporters of the theory of value.

What is needed to establish factories in an agricultural state? First, land is required for workshops and houses. Water power is generally also necessary. More than enough land and water power are available in a purely agrarian country. The landowner who sells land to a manufacturer will doubtless secure a higher price than he could have hoped to obtain if the land had been sold for agricultural purposes.

To erect factories, workshops, and dwellings the manufacturer needs stone, sand, lime and timber. All these are of little or no value in a purely agricultural country but now they suddenly do have a value and a landowner can make a handsome profit by selling them.

Builders and factory workers consume food, while machines consume fuel. There is normally a surplus both of food and fuel in an agrarian country. The sale of such commodities stimulates the agrarian economy.

The factory owner uses wool, hemp, flax, vegetable oils, and dyestuffs. All these products are generally available in an agricultural country in far greater quantities than they are consumed. If these commodities were sent abroad and then imported again in the form of manufactured products far more warehouses would be needed than if they were manufactured in local factories.

Thus a country which grows its own cereals and then turns the

---

society, must bear a certain proportion to the whole capital of that society, and never can exceed that proportion. No regulation of commerce can increase the quantity of industry in any society beyond what its capital can maintain. It can only divert part of it into a direction into which it might not otherwise have gone; and it is by no means certain that this artificial direction is likely to be more advantageous to the society than that into which it would have gone of its own accord.

Every individual is continually exerting himself to find out the most advantageous employment for whatever capital he can command. It is his own advantage, indeed, and not that of the society, which he has in view. But the study of his own advantage naturally, or rather necessarily, leads him to prefer that employment which is most advantageous to the society.

grain into flour and the flour into bread does not need to keep cereals stored in warehouses as would be necessary if the cereals were sent to England to be turned into flour and then imported again in processed form. The new factories do not deprive agriculture of either natural resources or supplies of cereals.

What then can agriculture lose? Intellectual capital? Very little intellectual capital exists in a purely agricultural country and if it did exist it would not be lost. In the early stages of industrialisation the necessary technical knowledge and skill must come from abroad (and not from local agriculture).

Is labour lost? No. There is a surplus of labour in all agricultural societies and the workers are relatively uneducated. Moreover factories provide employment for a type of labour that is useless on the land – namely the labour of women, children, and old people.

But if one assumes that the factories will create a considerable demand for labour it is also reasonable to assume that this will bring about a general rise in wages. While on the one hand landowners and farmers have to pay higher wages, they will on the other hand receive higher prices for the products that they sell to manufacturers. Moreover agricultural production will increase because the workers on the land are better paid and better fed. So the production of manufactured goods by the factories is a pure gain to society.

The significance of this fact – taken in conjunction with our previous observations – will become clear if one thinks of all those who work on the land as a single family engaged in a joint productive enterprise.[1]

It would surely be foolish for a country to fail to harness its waterfalls, or to let its minerals lie undisturbed in the earth, or to export raw materials and foodstuffs in return for manufactured goods of one tenth of their value. It would be folly for a society to allow most of its physical and intellectual resources to rot in idleness.

1. [List's note] The author considers that he should make it clear that he does not support the doctrines of the St Simonians. He does not believe in the possibility of establishing large communities in which property is held in common – at any rate in the present state of human society. Nevertheless the suggestion that we have made is correct. It is often possible to simplify the most abstruse economic problems if one thinks of a state as a single family, the members of which are not divided by private interests. On this assumption what is useful and advantageous – or harmful and disadvantageous – for society as a whole will be the same for its individual members.

It is obvious that what a country needs to become industrialised is an adequate labour force – easily available from the land – which will have to be taught technical skills and new habits of work. It is clear that industrialisation will not involve any loss of capital by agriculture, except what is needed to buy foreign machinery. On the contrary industrialisation will greatly increase the value of a country's natural resources.

It is astonishing that the exponents of the theory of value have for so long confused so clear a matter. It is still more surprising that the cosmopolitan economists have managed to keep silent concerning the great advantages of the policy of protection although it is self-evident that a system of tariffs safeguards industry and promotes the welfare of society. In England, the most advanced industrial country in the world, the policy of protection has safeguarded capital, technical knowledge, and skilled labour. People are attracted to a country which safeguards its industries by the policy of protection because they wish to share in the advantages provided by tariffs. This migration of foreign resources – physical and intellectual capital – is certainly not a gain made at the expense of a country's agriculture.

It cannot be denied that only advanced civilised countries – where a man is recompensed for leaving his homeland by the guarantee of personal freedom and the protection of his property – can hope to become industrialised by attracting English capital and technical knowledge.

The arguments that we have advanced are no mere abstract propositions. They are based upon established facts. All countries in which, under favourable circumstances, industries have been established through the policy of protection, have found that agriculture has gained amazingly in strength simply through the erection and operation of factories. Again, in a country in which canals and railways are built it is agriculture which first secures the most obvious advantage from these public works – a recompense for having, to a great extent, paid for them.[1]

1. [List's note] Adam Smith writes in Book IV, chapter 9 (of *The Wealth of Nations*):

> According to this liberal and generous system, therefore, the most advantageous method in which a landed nation can raise up artificers, manufacturers and merchants of its own, is to grant the most perfect freedom of trade to the artificers, manufacturers and merchants of all other nations. It thereby raises the

Does the Protection of Industry by a Tariff give Manufacturers a Monopoly prejudicial to the Consumers of the Goods that they make?

MONOPOLY! That dread word has often been used in the last century to brand the alleged despotic schemes of financiers which have occasioned great public calamities.

Merchants produce nothing. They make a living by buying and selling goods. It is in their interest to denounce any measure that

---

value of the surplus produce of its own land, of which the continual increase gradually establishes a fund, which in due time necessarily raises up all the artificers, manufacturers and merchants whom it has occasion for.

When a landed nation on the contrary, oppresses either by high duties or by prohibitions the trade of foreign nations, it necessarily hurts its own interest in two different ways. First, by raising the price of all foreign goods and of all sorts of manufactures, it necessarily sinks the real value of the surplus produce of its own land, with which, or what comes to the same thing, with the price of which, it purchases those foreign goods and manufactures. Secondly by giving a sort of monopoly of the home market to its own merchants, artificers, and manufacturers, it raises the rate of mercantile and manufacturing profit in proportion to that of agricultural profit, and consequently either draws from agriculture a part of the capital which had before been employed in it, or hinders from going to it a part of what would otherwise have gone to it. This policy, therefore, discourages agriculture in two different ways, first by sinking the real value of its produce, and thereby lowering the rate of its profit; and, secondly, by raising the rate of profit in all other employments. Agriculture is rendered less advantageous, and trade and manufactures more advantageous than they otherwise would be; and every man is tempted by his own interest to turn, as much as he can, both his capital and his industry from the former to the latter employments.

Though, by this oppressive policy, a landed nation should be able to raise up artificers, manufacturers and merchants of its own, somewhat sooner than it could do by the freedom of trade; a matter, however, which is not a little doubtful; yet it would raise them up, if one may say so, prematurely, and before it was perfectly ripe for them. By raising up too hastily one species of industry, it would depress another more valuable species of industry ...

[At the beginning of the quotation List omits the words: "According to this liberal and generous system, therefore ..."]

hampers their freedom to buy and to sell. Merchants have condemned as a "monopoly" any system of protection that is introduced in a country to safeguard the home market in manufactured goods for citizens of that country.

Is it really right to attack as a "monopoly" a measure to ensure that our 20 million industrialists enjoy a legal right to supply our 20 million agriculturalists with manufactured goods – especially when one remembers that our agriculturalists enjoy a natural monopoly to supply our 20 million industrialists with foodstuffs?

The policy of protection confers no privilege on one citizen at the expense of another. The privilege is one enjoyed by a whole nation at the expense of another nation. All manufacturers who are citizens of a country enjoy the same rights in the home market of a country as their fellow citizens. Only in that special sense can a tariff be said to confer a "monopoly".

There are useful and just monopolies as well as harmful and unjust monopolies. Thus a useful and just monopoly is one granted to an inventor who enjoys the exclusive use of his discovery for a definite period of time. The reason for granting a monopoly of this kind is self-evident and requires no further elucidation.

A similar motive lies behind the granting of a monopoly in the home market to all manufacturers who are citizens of the country. Such a monopoly is not given to any individual at the expense of society as a whole. The privilege of tariff protection is granted without exception to all industrialists who are citizens of the country. Anybody is free to set up a factory and anybody who does so is allowed to operate the factory as he pleases. The protection enjoyed by manufacturers eventually benefits the very people it is supposed to harm – namely those who work on the land.

The granting of exclusive privileges in the home market to industrialists is open to criticism only if those privileges cause manufactured goods to be always sold at a higher price than similar goods made abroad.

But when a country's industries have developed to such an extent that they can face foreign competition in the home market, it will be found – as we have shown in chapter 11 – that the goods made at home will be cheaper than those made abroad. This satisfactory state of affairs will be due partly to tariff protection in the past and partly to foreign competition.

The social and political conditions of some countries have not developed sufficiently for there to be much internal competition between local manufacturers in the home markets. In such countries – and only in such countries – will the privileges enjoyed by manufacturers through the imposition of a tariff enable a handful of rich powerful firms to plunder the consumers. They can charge high prices for their goods. Only in these circumstances may the privileges granted to manufacturers be regarded as a dangerous monopoly which would hinder and slow down the development of a country's productive powers.

―――――――――

CHAPTER SIXTEEN

Are the Interests of Consumers sacrificed if the Home Market is dominated by native Manufacturers?

IN CHAPTER THIRTEEN we explained why a country in the second or third phase of industrialisation has not fully developed its manufacturing capacity. And we showed how the goods manufactured in such a country are necessarily lower in quality and higher in price than those produced in a fully industrialised country. In the circumstances it has been argued that the granting of tariff protection to manufacturers must inevitably involve some sacrifice on the part of consumers and must appear to be unfair to them.

To reply to this criticism of the policy of protection and to judge this policy in its true light we must first consider who, if anybody, is really harmed by the imposition of a tariff.

Manufactured goods are consumed by:

1. manufacturers themselves: one industrialist consumes goods produced by another industrialist.
2. those who live and work on the land,
3. the trading classes,

4. the capitalists and those who have private incomes,
5. the professional classes and the artists,
6. the civil servants.

We have already shown in chapter 12 that the higher prices charged for manufactured goods inflict no injury if one manufacturer is consuming the products made by another manufacturer. This is because no branch of industry can flourish unless all other branches of industry are also flourishing.

The majority of consumers in a society in the second or third phase of industrialisation are those who live and work on the land. There can be no doubt whatever that they have to pay higher prices for manufactured goods if tariffs are imposed upon those goods and if competition between local manufacturers has not yet been fully developed. But should the success or failure of an economic policy be judged solely by the prices charged for manufactured goods? Should one not also take into account what a man gets for the products that he sells? If he gets more for the products that he sells, than he pays for the goods that he buys, is he not prospering? Even if the money that he gets from what he sells just equals the money that he pays for his purchases, he may still be regarded as having prospered. Is the owner of a piece of land near Paris, who has to pay higher prices for the goods that he buys really in a worse position than the owner of a piece of land of equal extent, which is situated far from any town or factory? We have already explained in chapter 10 that if agriculture depends mainly upon foreign trade it is subject to serious fluctuations. We have explained in chapter 11 how great are the advantages to farming if national industries expand. We have also shown that the policy of protecting industry by tariffs, far from injuring agriculture, eventually confers the greatest benefits upon agriculture.

It is possible that, in the early stages of industrialisation, the introduction of import duties to foster manufacturing enterprises, may impose some sacrifices upon agriculture. But what are these sacrifices in comparison with the depressions in trade caused by commercial crises, political revolutions, foreign tariffs, or wars that inevitably afflict an economy that is almost entirely dependent upon foreign trade? In all countries in which industry has developed with the aid of tariffs, agriculture too has flourished. Does this not prove that any sacrifices imposed upon farming in the early stages of industrialisation – if they really can be called sacrifices – are of relatively small importance and indeed are hardly noticeable?

Even if one were prepared to admit that agriculture has to make some sacrifices in the early stages of industrialisation it would still be true to say that eventually agriculture will be richly compensated by an enormous – indeed a hundredfold – expansion of its output. This will happen as soon as industry has reached its highest peak of production. Then all the hard work, the sacrifices, and the anxieties of rearing this tender plant will reap its due reward. Eventually competition between industrialists themselves will cause a reduction in the prices of manufactured goods below those charged by foreign firms. As industry expands and as the population grows there will be an ever increasing demand for agricultural products so that the prices of farm produce will rise. This should prove to those who work on the land that they should not hesitate to make sacrifices now in order to prepare the way for the prosperity of future generations. This prosperity is illustrated by the case of a farmer who harvests fruit from his orchards and so benefits from the hard work of his ancestors who planted the trees. Those who work on the land have no reason to complain of the poor quality or the high cost of manufactured goods in the early stages of industrialisation when industries benefit from tariff protection.

This applies also to capitalists, to people with private incomes, to pensioners, to professional men, and to artists. These classes in society gain enormously when industry and agriculture flourish. This is self-evident and need not be discussed further.

Merchants, too, lose nothing if there is an increase in the output of the factories and farms. The production and the consumption of farmers and manufacturers will increase in the same proportion. The productive capacity of the agrarian and industrial sectors of the economy will also expand to the same degree. The merchants – mere intermediaries between producers and consumers – are not affected by these developments.

There can be no doubt that the internal commerce of a country which has reached the highest stage of industrialisation is much larger and much more significant than that of a purely agricultural country. It is equally certain that a fully industrialised country needs far more foreign raw materials and exports far more manufactured goods than a purely agrarian country.

The only people who are inconvenienced by the introduction of tariffs are the commission agents of foreign manufacturers and those who buy farm produce to sell abroad. They will merely lose the business which they have been accustomed to handle and which has been necessary in the past. But as industry develops so will the activities of these merchants and it will be easy for them to find some other outlet for their skill in business. Here too one cannot argue that their interests have really been injured by the introduction of tariffs.

Those who lose most through the introduction of the policy of protection are civil servants and all those whose salaries or incomes are not regulated by supply and demand. These people lose insofar as their salaries have been based upon lower prices. But the revenue of the state from taxes of all kinds will increase with the growth of a nation's productive powers and when this happens it will not be unreasonable to expect the taxpayers to accept an increase in the salaries of civil servants to bring those salaries into line with the increased cost of living.

CHAPTER SEVENTEEN

Is it necessary to protect Agriculture and, if so, in what Circumstances?

IN ALL COUNTRIES in which attempts – whether successful or not – have been made to stimulate the output of manufactured goods by imposing tariffs there has been a demand from those who work on the land for similar protection for themselves and these demands have generally been met to a greater or lesser degree.

Experience has unquestionably shown that economists have been right when they have observed that a rise or a fall in the population is directly linked with the rise or fall in the output of agricultural production. It does not matter whether the foodstuffs consumed by the population in question are produced at home or are imported from abroad. If the import of foodstuffs is hindered in any way it is clear that the greater the reduction in food imports, the greater must be the decline in the population. There is no increase in the food produced at home and any tendency for the population to expand is sharply checked.

In a country in which industry is protected and is developing rapidly so that it has achieved great prosperity, the manufactured goods which would have been imported but for the imposition of tariffs are now made at home. This benefits mainly the industrial part of the population. A highly industrialised country is capable of producing the wealth needed to support a much larger industrial population than would be possible for a purely agrarian country. Increased quantities of raw materials for the factories are needed by a growing industrial population. The increased imports of raw materials and foodstuffs are balanced by the export of manufactured or agricultural products of equal value. But this growth in the industrial population – and these exports – would be lost if any restrictions were placed on the importation of raw materials and foodstuffs.

In the last chapter, however, we showed that a country's agriculture can flourish only if its industry flourishes as well. It is clear therefore that any attempt to protect the home market for the benefit of the farming community by the imposition of a tariff would not produce the desired result but would actually harm agriculture.

Immediately after the imposition of a tariff designed to safeguard the interests of the agrarian sector of the economy it might appear as if some real benefits had been conferred upon agriculture. If the import of meat were prohibited or made very difficult by the imposition of a high import duty it might appear that cattle farmers would secure an immediate advantage. Soon, however, it would become apparent that the industrial part of the population was suffering owing to the high price of meat while the farmers were suffering from a reduction in their exports abroad. Foreigners who formerly exchanged their cattle for our wines and our manufactured goods would now leave us in the lurch. France has had this experience not only with regard to meat but also with regard to other products.[1] England has suffered in the past and will suffer still

---

1. [List's note] Charles Dupin observes in his *Forces productives et commerciales de la France* (two volumes, 1827), Part I, p. 116: "It would be far better to trade in complete freedom and to give up the stupid idea of protecting negligent, ignorant and

more in the future for failing to recognise the natural laws of exchange of agricultural products.

When considering the question of free trade one must appreciate that agriculture is in quite a different position from industry. No one can deny that most countries are potentially capable of establishing and developing all kinds of industries, assuming that they have reached a sufficiently advanced standard of civilisation. It is equally clear that agriculture is dependent upon natural processes that man can do little to modify. For this reason different countries and different regions specialise in growing different products such as grapes, cattle, sheep, cereals, timber, tobacco or cotton. Common sense tells us that it would be foolish to try and produce different products from those to which a region is best suited because of its climate and soil and because of the habits and skill of its inhabitants.

It is astonishing that the arguments of the doctrinaire cosmopolitan economists are, to a great extent, applied rigidly to agri-

---

idle French farmers from the competition of the active, keen, and efficient farmers living in territories adjacent to our frontiers. By doing that we would avoid the disagreeable retaliation of foreigners directed against our agriculture and our industry".

Chaptal (*De l'industrie françoise*, Vol. I, p. 196) gives the following estimate of the number of cattle in France:

Bulls	214,131
Oxen	1,701,740
Cows	3,909,959
	5,825,830

Before the import duties on cattle were increased the imports of cattle into France were:

Oxen	16,000
Cows	20,000
	36,000

Cattle imports therefore amounted to only one 160th of the total number of cattle in France. Obviously the closing of this insignificant import trade would not affect the prosperity of French agriculture in any way. The depressed state of farming around Paris and in certain departments in western France will decline still further. Workers, who are most in need of good food will suffer most and the working strength of the whole nation will be weakened. At the market in Poissy the average price of meat rose from 42 centimes to 50 centimes. This illustrates a new and very important distinction between the output of farming and the output of industry – a distinction that we have not mentioned previously. Different classes in society and different districts in a country are affected in different ways if high import duties are imposed upon foodstuffs whereas all classes and all parts of the country are equally affected if high import duties are levied upon manufactured goods.

culture. These economists have blundered by treating the output of agriculture in the same way as the output of industry although, as we have seen, the two forms of production are governed by quite different laws.

We propose to make this distinction clear because we wish to be strictly impartial and have no desire to be accused of being a partisan supporter of the factory owners.

It is in the nature of things that agriculture should generally have a natural monopoly of the home market. The position of industry is quite different.

As a country becomes more advanced and its industries expand those who work on the land have even less cause to fear competition in the home market from foreigners. The exact opposite is true of the factory owners.

Foreign competition can never totally destroy agriculture. The nature of agricultural production is such that if farmers can find no profitable outlet for their surplus produce at home or abroad they can make use of the surplus on their own farms by increasing their stock or by improving their land. It is far easier for a farmer than for a factory owner to wait for better times. Severe competition, however, spells certain ruin for the factory owner – and for his workers, machines, premises, and business organisation.

It costs little to train men to work on the land – nature takes care of that – and most of these workers need only a robust constitution and do not require a great deal of skill. The situation is quite different in industry.

If agriculturalists are forced by low prices to keep their produce in their barns they may for a time enjoy more food than they would do if high prices encouraged them to sell more of their produce. In the factories, on the other hand, competition – and consequent low prices – leads to a slump, unemployment, and universal distress.

If those who work on the land do not have enough money to pay for high quality factory goods, they can make their own manu-factured goods. The sacrifice may be unpleasant but it does not threaten his livelihood. But if the factory worker is short of food his health – often his very life – is threatened.

By protecting industry with tariffs a country will be able to attract foreign capital, entrepreneurs, skilled and unskilled workers, and machines. This either does not apply to agriculture at all or it applies to agriculture to only a very limited degree.

The output of factories is capable of an immense expansion but any increase in agricultural output is limited by the area of farm land that is available and by the nature of the soil and the climate.

Tariffs to protect manufactures directly stimulates the development of industry. On the other hand tariffs imposed to protect agriculture are very harmful to industry.

If the policy of protection for industry is maintained for a long time the competition in the home market between industrialists will lead to a continual fall in the prices of manufactured goods. On the other hand, the longer this protection continues, the more will the prices of farm products decline.

Tariffs to protect industry lead to an increase in the wages paid to factory workers. Tariffs to protect agriculture from foreign competition will neither increase the profits of tenant farmers nor the wages of farm labourers. Only the rents paid to landowners will increase. This will give the landed aristocracy of a country a monopoly at the expense of the vast majority of the inhabitants – the poorest, the most oppressed, and the most useful class – namely the working class in general, including the farm workers.

Protection by the imposition of a tariff enables factory owners to raise loans from capitalists. Only this protection gives the founder of a new factory the ability to secure for his undertaking the money with which to buy essential equipment. On the other hand the owner of land or property already possesses the security that he needs to raise loans.

To increase the cost of food by the imposition of prohibitions or import duties is to defy the natural law of national survival. It gives to those who already monopolise a country's land a second monopoly by permitting an artificial increase in the cost of agricultural produce which harms the welfare of society as a whole. On the other hand to protect industry by the imposition of a tariff provides the working class with jobs and with food and it enables it to escape from the consequences of any increase in the cost of manufactured goods.

Only the protection of industry by means of a tariff will enable a country to buy food from abroad if the harvest at home should fail. To stimulate regular imports – even to let foreigners know that imports may be needed in the future – will encourage foreign countries to produce a surplus of agricultural products and to store them so that they can be made available if required. A country which closes its frontiers to foreign raw materials and foodstuffs to protect its own agriculture will deprive itself of the possibility of getting food from abroad if its own harvest should fail. In addition it will discourage the expansion of farm produce in foreign countries.

By opening its frontiers freely to all agricultural products from abroad an industrial nation is ensured of foreign markets in which to sell its manufactured goods. But if it closes its frontiers to farm produce from abroad it will force foreign agricultural states to promote the development of their own industries.

The unrestricted import of raw materials and foodstuffs makes it possible for a country to establish colonies. A mutual trade between the mother country and its overseas possessions can be established which will be highly advantageous to both of them. But if a country prohibits the import of agricultural products it will discard a means by which it can become wealthy and provide work to some of its employed.

As we have already observed, the imposition of a tariff to protect industry is essential for the encouragement of cultural progress and for the maintenance of the power, independence, and prosperity of a nation. It is the only way to stimulate agriculture so that it can reach a peak of efficiency. But the imposition of a tariff to protect farming simply enriches some great landowners at the expense of others who make a living on the land.

For these reasons we believe that there should be complete freedom of trade between all nations with regard to raw materials and foodstuffs. Human society as a whole and all countries without exception will secure great advantages and great wealth from this policy. On the other hand universal free trade with regard to manufactured goods would deprive a number of countries of their independence, their power, and their standard of living and would make it impossible for them to make further progress towards a higher standard of civilisation.

It would perhaps be possible to find other important differences between the effects of prohibitions and import duties on manufactured goods and on agricultural products but we hope that the differences that we have already indicated will be sufficient for our purpose.

In view of the arguments that we have advanced it may be asked why in nearly all countries the agricultural interest has been able to secure the imposition of tariffs on foodstuffs and raw materials.

Manufacturers realise that to persuade a government to impose a general tariff they must secure the support of the agricultural interest so as to overcome the opposition both of merchants engaged in foreign trade and of doctrinaire economists. The agriculturalists fail to appreciate that by supporting the imposition of a general tariff – including import duties on raw materials and foodstuffs – they are pursuing a mistaken policy which will ultimately be detrimental to their own interests.

In most legislative bodies those who will benefit from an immediate rise in the value of land are either in a majority or at any rate carry considerable weight in the debates and in the decisions that are taken. These men sacrifice real future advantages for an apparent immediate financial gain.

CHAPTER EIGHTEEN

Agriculture and Industry in the Fourth Period of Economic Development

THREE PHASES in the development of agriculture have been discussed in previous chapters.
1. In the first phase agriculture is isolated from foreign trade.
2. In the second phase agriculture is influenced by foreign trade.
3. In the third phase a balance has been achieved between agriculture and industry so that most – if not all – of the output of agriculture is consumed in the country in which it is produced.

These three phases in the development of agriculture correspond to three stages in the growth of industry, namely
1. The first phase is one of self-sufficiency when landowners and farmers produce most of the manufactured goods that they require. It is a period when domestic craft industries are the only ones in a country.
2. The second phase is one in which important industries develop,

either in association with or in competition with imported manufactured goods. It is a period when industry begins to be established, despite competition from foreign rivals, either by paying lower wages than those paid by firms abroad, or because of particular local advantages that it enjoys.

3. The third phase is one in which a country's industries dominate the home market, though not always completely.

There is a fourth period of development for both agriculture and industry, in which either all the raw materials – or part of the raw materials and foodstuffs – that a country requires are imported from foreign countries. Manufactured goods are exported in exchange for the raw materials and foodstuffs.

It might appear paradoxical that agriculture should have reached a more advanced stage of development when a country imports raw materials and foodstuffs than when it monopolised the home market. But the truth of our assertion will be evident to readers of our earlier chapters.

A country which imports raw materials and foodstuffs is one which is expanding its industrial capacity. It is a country in which costs of production are declining and in which industrialists are able to produce far more manufactured goods than the home market can absorb.

Such a country is far better placed than it would be if it restricted the flow of raw materials and foodstuffs from abroad and artificially raised the prices of agricultural produce at home by imposing prohibitions and high duties on imports. Such a country can provide far more employment than agriculture alone can provide for factory managers, skilled workers, and merchants. Isolated houses give way first to villages, then to hamlets, then to little towns, and then to great cities which double and even treble their houses and population.[1]

The construction of new highways and canals leads to an increased demand for building materials, fuel, and consumer goods of

1. [List has seen for himself in the United States how rapid economic growth stimulated equally rapid urban growth. In 1829 he wrote: "Some time ago, after an absence of six months, I again visited Philadephia. I found quite new streets and suburbs. The reason for this was the phenomenal expansion of agriculture which had stimulated a demand for manufactured goods. These developments were fostered by the existence of many natural and artificial means of communication". F. List, *Mitteilungen aus Nordamerika* (1829), reprinted in F. List, *Werke*, Vol. III (Part 1), p. 133.]

all kinds. The growth of new villages and towns, providing fresh markets for farm produce, follows the opening up of quarries, kilns, coalmines, or peat works. Farmers can now buy coal or peat instead of trying to obtain them from their own land in a primitive fashion. Numerous workers are employed in erecting buildings of all kinds and in constructing roads and canals. The demands of these workers stimulate the output of the farms in the district.

Gardens are converted into building land; open fields are turned into vegetable gardens and orchards; meadows and woods come under the plough. These changes are brought about by the continually growing demand for more agricultural produce. Part of this demand may be met by imports from abroad but this will be only a small part of the total new demand for milk, eggs, butter, vegetables, potatoes, and fruit as well as for oats and straw for farm horses and riding horses. Above all meat, vegetable oils, and dyestuffs are in great demand. When communications have been improved and farmers have been brought into closer contact with their customers the farmers in a country will have a distinct advantage over their foreign competitors in the home market because foreigners will have to pay more for transport, storage, and insurance. Local farmers will therefore secure the lion's share of the local market in the products that we have mentioned.

By concentrating on these products the farmers will be able to increase their output, earn larger profits, and give employment to far more labourers than would be possible in the relatively backward types of farming characteristic of the earlier stages of agricultural development – when, for example, farms existed which did little more than breed draught animals.

If the government of a country were to adopt a policy of restricting imports of raw material and grain, it would be impossible for agriculture to reach the most advanced stage of development and it would also be impossible for the industrialists to increase the sale of their manufactured goods abroad.

It has been argued that it would be a mistake to allow industry to grow to such an extent that it became absolutely dependent upon imported raw materials and foodstuffs and upon foreign markets for the sale of its manufactured goods. It has been argued, too, that such a dependence upon foreign countries is dangerous because both imports of raw materials and foodstuffs and exports of manufactured goods may suffer from interruptions to trade owing to

93

commercial crises or to the hostile tariffs of foreign countries. There is no need for anyone to worry on this account. A nation which has reached the most advanced stage of industrial and agricultural development will never lack either the means or the power to overcome difficulties of that kind. Anyone who is afraid of the future because of trade slumps or hostile foreign tariffs is like a man who refuses to walk on two legs because he is afraid that he might wear them out.

CHAPTER NINETEEN

The Productive Powers of Commerce

DOMESTIC AND FOREIGN commerce affects the exchange of the output of agriculture and industry. Merchants seek markets where there is a demand for particular manufactured goods or farm produce. They arrange the necessary transport facilities and they are responsible for collecting debts due to producers. In addition they provide credit and arrange for the storage of products that cannot be sold immediately. In this way merchants assist in the process of production and help to maintain the balance between output and consumption. They are able to cope with the situation if the harvest is either too big or too small.

There are those who define trade as the link between producers and consumers. In fact merchants have two functions. First, as we have explained, they facilitate the exchange of the output of various branches of agriculture and industry. Secondly, they link those who produce material goods with those – for example, officials, artists and retired people – who are only consumers.

To appreciate fully the productive powers of commerce we must concentrate our attention upon the principal function of merchants which is to link the two main economic sectors – agriculture and industry. An examination of the functions of commerce leads us to draw the following conclusions:

1. Strictly speaking merchants are not producers. They only

foster the production and consumption of manufacturers and farmers.

2. Commerce expands and declines as industry and agriculture expand and decline.

3. If industry and agriculture flourish because their home market is protected, commerce flourishes to the same extent. It can be proved that internal trade is from five to ten times as great as foreign trade in a country in which industry and agriculture have reached an advanced stage of development.

4. Only insofar as foreign commerce promotes a country's industry and agriculture can it be allowed to operate freely. Only in those circumstances can it be considered useful to a country's economic development.

5. It has been shown that foreign trade can sometimes have harmful effects upon the development of a country's agriculture and industry. When that happens a country would injure its own economic interests if it failed to check these harmful effects by imposing suitable restrictions upon foreign commerce.

6. In a country in which industry has reached an advanced stage of development, internal trade is far more important than foreign trade. And foreign trade expands or declines as the industry of a nation expands or declines. As we have shown in earlier chapters, common sense tells us – and the experience of all countries confirms the fact – that the growth of a nation's industries is accompanied by a corresponding expansion of its imports of raw materials and foodstuffs and its exports of manufactured goods. In a predominantly agricultural country – even if complete free trade has been established – the total value of foreign trade is quite insignificant in comparison with the value of the imports and exports of a highly industrialised country, even if that country has placed tariff restrictions upon foreign commerce.

7. By expanding and developing its industries a country can increase its independence, power, and prosperity. When this happens it is above all foreign trade that benefits. The very existence of trade with other countries depends upon the protection which the government is able to give it against foreign rivals. The foreign trade of a country faces ruin if it cannot rely upon support from a strong national government.

8. In the absence of a growing industry and in the absence of government support the foreign trade of a nation – like other

aspects of the economy – is left to the tender mercies of any foreign country that chooses to take arbitrary action against it. In these circumstances foreign commerce is defenceless against such arbitrary acts and – even in peacetime – can become virtually a sort of satellite dependency of a foreign power.

9. In wartime the trade between belligerents is completely destroyed and utterly ruined. Merchant ships lie at anchor in their harbours, merchant seamen seek employment abroad, and master mariners find work on the land. The capital invested in foreign trade either earns no profits or is transferred abroad. Merchants who invest their capital in factories which prosper because of the war find themselves in a paradoxical position. The very men who before the war sang the praises of free trade now that hostilities have ceased find themselves supporting the introduction of a tariff to safeguard the capital that they have invested in manufacturing enterprises. An advanced industrial state, however, is in quite a different position with regard to foreign trade. Supported by a strong navy, such a country will soon find new markets abroad to replace those which have been lost for the time being. And even if some capital, formerly devoted to foreign trade, can no longer find profitable employment abroad, there are a thousand opportunities for new safe advantageous investments in prosperous local industries at home.

10. Merchants engaged simply in transit trade have both feet in foreign states and their activities need to be considered only if they stimulate home industries, only if the commissions that they earn are used for the benefit of the country as a whole, and only if one can hope that the profits which they earn will one day benefit the nation. Compared with internal commerce one should always regard foreign trade as an alien intruder in the national economy. Merchants engaged in foreign trade should never expect a government to favour their views and aspirations. Least of all should they expect the state to make any sacrifices on their behalf.

In view of what has been said it is clear that there is really no clash of interests as far as commerce, agriculture and industry are concerned. Merchants have no right to put forward claims for special treatment, which would be injurious to a country's agriculture or industry. It is quite unreasonable to regard freedom of trade in an isolated fashion as if commerce were an independent factor in the economic process. In fact commerce is no more than a link between the various productive forces in society.

No clearer proof of our argument can be given than the one already put forward in chapter 14 where we suggested that a country should be regarded as a united society in which goods belong to all its members. If this point of view is accepted, we can ask the question: To what extent can merchants be regarded as producers in view of the fact that they are concerned simply with recording, storing, dispatching and distributing goods? Will their business not increase to the same extent as the output of agriculture and industry? Would not the merchants themselves condemn a country for its folly if it exported wool and imported woollen cloths containing only a quarter of the raw wool sent in exchange? Would not the merchants admit that it would be just as foolish and reckless to export cereals and to import flour and bread in return? Would not such a policy be even more foolish if the manpower and the skill were available to establish cloth mills and if agriculture produced a surplus of food with which to feed the factory workers? Could the merchants who formerly exported wool and imported cloth have the slightest justification for criticising the government for bringing these harmful transactions to an end? And if they did put forward such an argument one would give the following reply: The industry of a country can produce four times as much cloth in its own factories as was formerly imported. In this situation the merchants will benefit because there will be a very substantial increase in the registering, the dispatching, and the distribution of goods at home because everybody will be consuming twice as much cloth as before. In addition half of the cloth will be worth twice as much as the wool that was formerly sent abroad. The country will gain not only by exporting cloth but it will also gain twice as much as before from its imports. This is because it will be possible to export cloth in exchange for goods twice the value of those formerly imported in exchange for raw wool. It follows that the merchants engaged in the export-import business are not to be regarded as useless members of society. On the contrary, in the circumstances that we have mentioned, their usefulness to society has actually doubled.

There is only one case in which export-import merchants would have a right to object to measures taken to protect industry. This is if a nation does not yet have a sufficient manpower to produce the wool or to manufacture cloth successfully in comparison with the country from which it has been accustomed to buy cloth in exchange for wool. In such circumstances the nation would no doubt be better clothed if, at any rate for the time being, it continued to produce wool and to exchange it for cloth.

This is so obvious that the failure of merchants to appreciate the situation would be truly astonishing were it not for the fact that the interests of commerce in general are very often different from the interests of individual merchants. In our next chapter we propose to discuss this difference and to elucidate its results. At this point, however, we wish to guard against any suggestion that we have failed to be objective by stating categorically that we fully appreciate the importance of commerce for the development of a country's productive powers and cultural progress.

It is by commerce that new products appear on the market and that new demands for consumer goods are created. To secure these goods primitive peoples become accustomed to work and this in turn leads to progress in morality, religion and law. It is the merchant and not the missionary who stimulates backward primitive peoples in their advance towards a more civilised existence.

It is the merchant who fosters the development of agriculture which, but for his efforts, would continue to languish in the most miserable fashion. It is he who prepares people to enter a new stage of economic and social existence. It is his efforts which strike at the very roots of prejudice, fanaticism, physical and intellectual idleness, the harmful privileges of nobles, and the arbitrary rule of despots. He gives primitive peoples the will and the ability to improve themselves, because he provides them with new goods and so awakens in them the desire to make these goods themselves. He also provides them with the means to introduce and to develop their own domestic industries.

Only during the transition from the second to the third stage of agriculture do the activities of certain merchants clash with the interests of society as a whole. In the fourth stage of agriculture, however, the interests of merchants and of society once more coincide.

In the early stages of economic development, commerce encourages the growth of a country's productive powers and helps to bring them into closer association with each other. Later on commerce will actually succeed in completely uniting a nation's productive powers.

Free trade is no idle dream. With the triumph of reason it will be universally established and then all peoples on earth will achieve the highest degree of physical and cultural well being. This, however, can happen only when all countries have reached the same stage in their economic, moral, social, and political development. Moreover it would appear that if the world is divided into large national units, this process of unification will be hastened to a successful conclusion.

CHAPTER TWENTY

How do the Interests of Commerce differ from the Interests of Individual Merchants?

ONLY THOSE who work on the land or in industry produce something that did not previously exist. Their activities are therefore necessarily always beneficial to society as a whole. (There is one exception to this.) The interests of particular producers may be very seriously injured if their output is too large and if a surplus of goods is thereby created. A temporary slump occurs whenever the supply of a particular product exceeds the demand.

A merchant's business is not affected in the same way. He himself produces no consumer goods. He simply gives a value to existing goods by bringing them to market. His object is simply to make money by exchanging products and it is quite immaterial to him if this exchange harms the productive powers of a nation or of the whole world.

But a merchant should not be criticised for being indifferent to the harm that he may inflict upon a nation's productive powers because these activities are an integral part of his business. It is in the nature of things that he must buy in the cheapest market and sell in the dearest. If all the farmers in a country decided to dig up their fruit trees and to export them, no merchant would have any scruples in handling the transaction, always provided that a profit could be made on the deal. Indeed, if it were possible, he would export the very soil in which the trees were growing. And having looted the last scrap of earth he would take ship to another country and continue his business there.

A merchant would have no scruples in selling factories to foreigners. In the event of a slump a merchant – true to the principle of buying in the cheapest market and selling in the dearest – would be quite capable of raising capital by selling an industrial enterprise in his own country and using the money by buy cheaply in a foreign country goods that their owners were forced to sell as trade was depressed. The merchant could then dump these goods in his own country and condemn thousands of workers to unemployment and starvation. The tragic consequences of his actions would cause him little concern. As a supporter of the theory of value he carries on his business with the sole object of making a profit at the end of the year. If he feels it necessary to excuse his conduct he resorts to a platitude and simply argues that the misfortunes that he has helped to bring about are due to circumstances beyond his control.

If he cannot profit from his country's prosperity a merchant will speculate on its misfortunes such as famine or war. He profits from the export of beasts essential for farming. He profits from the sale of the machinery and stock of bankrupt industrial enterprises. He profits from the emigration of factory managers, and unemployed urban and rural workers. He even profits from the sale of arms to his country's enemies. He speculates and makes money by engaging in all these dubious activities. He poisons entire nations and communities with his brandy and still continues to proclaim his adherence to the policy of "laissez faire et laissez passer".

A true story is told of a pious Quaker, well known for his high moral sentiments and sound religious principles. When his ship was captured and was found to be packed with arms for the enemy, the captain who had taken him prisoner rebuked him for his lack of patriotism. The Quaker angrily replied: "What do you mean, Sir? I am a merchant and I would go to hell if my business took me there." That is how the mind of a merchant works. Neither religion nor morality can change his true character.

It is in the very nature of things that a merchant should defend absolutely unrestricted freedom of trade in this way, even if his actions are utterly at variance with the interests of commerce in general. If a fox were a member of a legislative assembly he would protest that it would be an infringement of natural law to pass a bill forbidding the consumption of poultry and pigeons.

100

The merchant appeals to "natural law" to condemn anything which hampers his business. He thinks that there is nothing wrong in a man of honour engaging in smuggling. Indeed he actually flatters himself that contraband trade is a proper and honourable way of enforcing the "natural law" that society has broken.

To such an extent are merchants debased by their determination to make a profit at any cost that not only individuals but groups of merchants – such as shipowners, shipbuilders, and insurance companies – will unite to make money out of the thousands of people and the millions of francs worth of goods that are lost at sea every year. These men are thieves and robbers.

It will need the intervention of a statesman of high character to ensure that any clash of interests between the mercantile community on the one hand and a nation, society, or humanity on the other is resolved in favour of the latter.

It has been repeatedly observed that merchants engaged in foreign trade will inevitably side with their country's enemies as soon as they see that such a course of action will benefit them financially.

A merchant, unlike a philosopher, is no citizen of the world. If his own country sinks into a wretched and shameful state of bankruptcy and slavery, a merchant will take himself off to a foreign country with all his possessions. Merchants deserted Venice, Portugal, and the Hansa Towns as soon as these states declined. Adam Smith has no illusions concerning the behaviour of merchants (see Book III, chapter 4).[1]

Measures of state control designed to maintain the quality of manufactured goods which are exported are advantageous to commerce in general but they are detested by individual merchants who complain bitterly of any interference in their business and reiterate their demand for a policy of "laissez faire et laissez passer". Commerce in general obviously benefits from canals and railways and

1. [The passage which List had in mind was probably the following: "A merchant, it has been said very properly, is not necessarily the citizen of any particular country. It is in a great measure indifferent to him from what place he carries on his trade; and a very trifling disgust will make him remove his capital, and together with it all the industry which it supports, from one country to another. No part of it can be said to belong to any particular country, until it has been spread as it were over the face of that country, either in buildings or in the lasting improvement of land ... The ordinary revolutions of war and government easily dry up the sources of that wealth which arises from commerce only" (*The Wealth of Nations,* Vol. I, pp. 373-4 (Everyman edition)).]

merchants normally are strongly in favour of their construction. But he loses all interest in the project as soon as he becomes a shareholder in a canal company or a railway company. Now he is interested only in making a profit from a rise in the value of his shares.

It is evident that a yawning chasm frequently exists between the interests of a particular merchant and the interests of commerce in general. One cannot strike a balance of commercial gains and loss from a national point of view by examining the profits and losses of individual merchants. Indeed commerce in general can be threatened and can be destroyed root and branch although at the same time some of the merchants engaged in foreign trade are making handsome profits. While commerce flourishes if a nation's productive powers are growing, an individual merchant prospers by making money, and – as we have seen – he can actually profit from the decline and fall of his native country.

It is by confusing the theory of productive powers with the theory of value that economists, who support free trade, have taken over the merchants' principle: Laissez faire et laissez passer. As we have shown in chapter 19 the principle should often be reversed. The more foreign manufactured goods fall in price during a slump, the more dangerous – in the national interest – is it to buy them owing to the danger of ruining our own factories. In such circumstances it is vitally important to levy high import duties on these products. Merchants on the whole demand "freedom" in the very widest sense – illegal and harmful freedom as well as lawful and useful freedom. But, in comparison with manufacturers, they cannot do very much to promote the development of freedom and the progress of science.

It is in the very nature of things that a manufacturer should sharpen his intellect by making a thorough study of the business in which he is engaged. And he takes a real interest in the progress of science, technology, and art. A merchant, on the other hand, concentrates upon arithmetic, double entry, and the state of the stock market and these are topics which are hardly likely to elevate the spirit or improve the intellect.

The interests of those who work on the land or in the factories are identical with those of the entire nation but the closer a merchant lives to a frontier the more is he drawn towards a foreign country. A merchant becomes a true citizen of his country only when he owns land or property or a factory or when he becomes associated with some industrial enterprise.

One of the main reasons why a merchant always opposes the imposition of any import duty is his great reluctance to give up a branch of business with which he is familiar and to embark upon a new sort of business with which he is not familiar.

But the very merchant who argues that it is difficult and inconvenient to make such a change does not hesitate to tell an unemployed factory operative that he ought to find work on the land, although this is undoubtedly much more difficult to do than it is for a merchant to transfer his capital from foreign trade to commerce and industry at home.

The most remarkable characteristic of the merchant who is mainly involved in the sort of commercial transactions that endanger the productive powers of his country and who is the sworn enemy of monopolies, privileges, restrictions and tariffs to protect what he calls "private industry" is the very person who leaves no stone unturned to secure for himself such aids from the state as soon as they happen to coincide with their own private interests.

He insists that the interests of the fishing industry must be safeguarded by premiums and by other measures of protection. He loudly demands the passing of Navigation Acts whenever foreign competition appears to threaten the prosperity of a country's mercantile marine. He appeals to his government to send gunboats to every sea to protect his ships from pirates and from hostile foreign merchants. He calls for the appointment of ambassadors in every foreign capital and of consuls in every foreign port to watch over his trading interests.

He cannot deny that a navigation code has turned the smallest sea power into the largest and most formidable in the world and he uses this fact to support his demand that his own government should adopt a navigation code. Yet at the same time he is quite capable of denouncing as unlawful and ineffective any attempt of the state to bring prosperity to industry by establishing a tariff. He seems unable to grasp the fact that a navigation code imposes severe restrictions, while premiums and import duties which protect the fishing industry are no different in principle from a tariff which protects industry.

There are merchants who demand that a government should devote the greater part of the budget to the maintenance of a fleet, but who also complain bitterly that it is scandalous to spend a lot of money in setting up an efficient customs administration which – so they say – is as absurd as it is harmful to the welfare of the state. Merchants engaged in smuggling have the effrontery to declare that the existence of a contraband trade proves that tariffs are not only ineffective but also unnecessary.

Their private interests turn merchants into citizens of the world and they make common cause with universal philosophers against a nation's own industries. These are strange bedfellows indeed.

Once more we reject the criticism that we have drawn a caricature of the truth. It is our intention to stick to the truth. We have described the merchant as he really is, as he can be, and as indeed he must necessarily be – unless a country deliberately sets limits to his lust for gain.

Merchants are the most faithful disciples of the theory of value. They invented the principles "laissez faire et laissez passer" and "buy where you can buy in the cheapest market". The cosmopolitan economists find that merchants are their most ardent followers and spread their doctrines with the greatest enthusiasm.

And so the doctrines of Adam Smith and Say must be regarded as the true "mercantile system" – an economic theory which places the interests of those merchants who import foreign manufactured goods above those of commerce in general. It is a theory which stresses only material wealth and ignores productive powers. It is a doctrine which sacrifices a country's future economic power, political greatness, and cultural progress in order to deceive people into believing in the "truth" of a principle which is in fact based upon the most despicable egotism.

It is indeed strange that those who most passionately denounce what they choose to call the mercantile system have in fact invented a real mercantile system all of their own – a system which exalts the hawker of foreign goods and actually includes the activities of the smuggler in the science of economics.

CHAPTER TWENTY ONE

Protection by Means of a Tariff[1]

THE ADVANTAGES of tariffs are as follows: They awake the spirit of enterprise in a country. They encourage young people to attend technical schools and to travel abroad to complete their studies. They encourage workers to give up existing jobs and to devote themselves for the rest of their lives to a new occupation – after first acquiring the necessary skills – even though success in the new job cannot be guaranteed. Tariffs safeguard the industrial enterprises of entrepreneurs who take risks and have no means of knowing if they are going to be a success or not. Tariffs encourage capitalists, manufacturers and skilled workers to migrate to our country bringing with them their money, machinery, and technical knowledge. Tariffs enable new factories to reach at a stroke the same degree of efficiency as most advanced enterprises abroad. They make it possible for these factories to make goods of as high quality as those produced in more advanced industrial countries. Tariffs give to entrepreneurs as large markets and as many customers as those enjoyed by foreign factory owners.

The drawbacks of tariffs are that they create thousands of customs officials in our frontiers; they restrict complete freedom of trading; and they impose upon citizens the inconvenience of having their premises searched. Even in time of peace tariffs stop friendly foreign countries from sending us their manufactured goods as if they were infectious diseases. And to some extent tariffs lower the moral standards of those who live near a frontier by putting temptation in their way to break the law. If anyone could suggest how the advantages of a tariff can be secured without the drawbacks we would be delighted to support such a proposal.

1. [List's note] Say writes as follows on tariffs (*Traité*, Part I, p. 251): "What would one say if customs duties were levied on clothes and shoes at every front door so as to force the happy householder to make these things for himself? ... That is the tariff system pushed to its logical conclusion". Our comment is that a nation is no shoemaker.

Unfortunately the advantages of a tariff can be secured only if we are prepared to put up with the drawbacks. There are many ways in which industrialisation can be promoted. They include the establishment of technical schools; the granting of financial assistance to enable scientists to travel abroad; the holding of industrial exhibitions at which new inventions can be shown; the establishment of companies to promote industry and internal commerce by regulating rivers and by constructing highways, canals, railways and steamships; the granting of honours to those who advance scientific knowledge or establish new industries; the payment of generous subsidies for new industries, new processes, new plants, and new efficient factories; and the granting of state loans to industrial enterprises. But all these measures will have little effect unless they are supported by a tariff.

Do not attempt to refute these arguments by pointing to Switzerland (which has developed its industries without a high national tariff). The great security of persons and property and the considerable measure of political freedom have for centuries favoured the development of industries in that country. Although in comparison with modern constitutional developments this freedom may appear to be somewhat out of date it has nevertheless enabled Switzerland to enjoy certain economic advantages which its neighbours have – to their cost – not enjoyed.

Moreover the reformation in Switzerland to some extent stimulated advances in industry, education, morality, thrift, and other aspects of human progress. The existence of political and religious freedom has enabled Switzerland to attract the money and the skill of persecuted Germans, Frenchmen and Italians. And the great reserves of capital – material and intellectual – which Switzerland has acquired over the centuries have never been dissipated by wars, persecution, despotism or high taxes.

Stimulated and developed by political and religious freedom, the spirit of enterprise and competition in Switzerland – coupled with the influence of society, family, and schools – has enabled those who could not make a good living at home to succeed abroad in any enterprise that they might undertake. With new skills at their disposal and with plenty of money in their pockets they would eventually return to the open skies and the mountains of their native land, where Swiss industry and society would gather the fruits of their sojourn abroad.

Since nature has not blessed Switzerland with a rich soil, her skilled and unskilled workers have been forced to seek their fortunes abroad and a considerable part of the population has been encouraged to devote itself to industrial pursuits. On the other hand Switzerland has been blessed with low wages, modest taxes, and a superfluity of water power. Much foreign capital has been invested in the country and many immigrants, from all parts of the world, have brought their knowledge and skill with them. All this has greatly stimulated the industrial development of Switzerland.

The growth of manufactures in Switzerland has also been stimulated by the profitable exchange of Swiss industrial products for the raw materials and foodstuffs of neighbouring countries. Moreover it has been easy for the Swiss to ignore the prohibitions of adjacent states and to smuggle their manufactured goods across their frontiers.

Much of Switzerland's output of industrial and agricultural products has been protected from foreign competition by the activities of gilds and other corporations, by the simplicity and stability of the manners and customs of the people – free from the bad influence of the luxurious courts of princes and nobles – and by the existence of a traditional way of life that has survived for centuries.

Commerce both at home and abroad has been stimulated by the ability of the Swiss to speak the languages of all their neighbours. They have been able to use new machinery and processes originating in these countries. Finally it may be observed that the money brought into the country by the many travellers who visit Switzerland contributes to the welfare not only of the rural population but of the whole country.

Tariffs are doubtless a very great nuisance but they should be regarded as the lesser of two evils, just as the maintenance of a standing army, the construction of fortresses and war itself are lesser evils when compared with the loss of a people's sovereignty and nationhood.

We repeat what we have observed in chapter 10. The imposition of a tariff should not be regarded as something discovered by economists or bureaucrats. It should be seen as the natural and inevitable consequences of international tensions and rivalries. There are despotic rulers whose sole object in life is to promote the growth of their political and financial power, without caring how much their subjects suffer. These despots have been forced to impose tariffs and to follow the same policy as democratic governments freely elected by all the voters. Such administrations find that they have no option but to adopt the policy of protection so as to cope with a situation in which the home market has for a long time been dominated by foreign competitors. And this has been done despite the fact that American economists, almost without exception, have strongly advocated the merits of the cosmopolitan doctrine of free trade. The Americans, like the Germans, have appreciated that they cannot move forward a single step without the aid of a tariff and the doctrinaire economists have been forced to eat their words to such an extent that their theories eventually collapse in irreconcilable contradictions.

Even Britain, the leading industrial state in the world – which would derive the greatest advantage if universal free trade were adopted – has not been persuaded by her cosmopolitan economists to give up the policy of tariff protection. Her excuse to foreign governments is that the revenues raised from existing import duties are not sufficient to meet the requirements of the budget, but debates in Parliament make it clear that all recent changes in the tariff have been motivated by a desire to protect English industries. Other countries – duped into lowering their import duties – have discovered after careful reflection how ridiculous is Britain's excuse for not adopting free trade. Foreign governments realise that as far as they are concerned it hardly matters why Britain reduces her purchases from abroad. It may be to secure a favourable balance of trade or it may be to strangle the growth of foreign industries. But she will still draw a large revenue from import duties.

On the other hand in the existing state of international trade it is the policy of protection that will eventually lead to the establishment of free trade. This is apparently a paradox but it is true. Experience shows that highly industrialised nations always – or nearly always – abuse their superior position in relatively backward countries. So long as the less advanced countries do not object to this shameful treatment, the arrogance of the advanced nation will know no bounds. But as soon as the weaker states begin to defend themselves the more powerful nation will adopt a more reasonable policy. Experience tells us that the bully who gets a thick ear from his victim soon changes his tune.

A tariff is not only a method of protecting home industries. It is also a weapon with which a nation can defend itself against every arbitrary aggression on the part of foreign states. A nation which is protected by a tariff can defend itself by threatening to retaliate if it is in danger of being harmed by the economic policy of another country. Such a threat will lead to the immediate removal of the danger or it will lead to the conclusion of a commercial treaty which will regulate the trade of the two countries to the advantage of both.

CHAPTER TWENTY TWO

Tariffs: Prohibitions and Duties on Imports and Exports

THERE ARE TWO methods by which industry may be safeguarded from foreign competition. One is to stop the importation of foreign raw materials, foodstuffs, and manufactured goods altogether. The other is to impose such high duties upon imports that native industrialists are given a distinct advantage over foreign competitors.

The first method of safeguarding industry is the most efficient method of achieving the desired result, provided that a check is maintained upon products which have already entered the country and are in circulation. But this has a serious drawback because the personal freedom of the individual is violated when customs officials search his home for contraband. It is also alleged that this type of protection stifles competition at home and encourages slackness among manufacturers. The second safeguard for manufacturers – the imposition of import duties rather than prohibitions – has the advantage that it permits sufficient quantities of foreign goods to enter the country to allow people to buy certain products not made at home and to encourage some competition between native and foreign manufacturers. This method of safeguarding the interests of manufacturers does not disturb the exchange of goods within a country and saves people from the risk of having their homes searched for contraband. The first method of safeguarding industry is called the "prohibitive system" while the second is called the "policy of protection".

Which of these two systems is the best? In this there can be no doubt that in the long run the prohibitive system is much less harmful than the system of protection. It is true that a failure to engage in foreign trade at all deprives a nation of the many advantages to be derived from having commercial contacts with other countries. A state which adopted the prohibitive system would be behaving in just as unreasonable a fashion as a hermit who cuts himself off from all contacts with his fellows.

In practice, however, the situation is quite different. We have already explained that the introduction of the prohibitive system is generally the result of a war and has nothing to do with theories advanced by economists. The prohibitive system ensures the continuation in peacetime of a state of affairs that previously existed when two countries were at war. If a war has lasted for a long time the industry of a country will have expanded considerably. Much capital will have been invested in new factories which will be giving employment to large numbers of workers. Millions of people will have invested their savings, their skills – indeed their whole future – in various branches of industry. The whole industrial strength of the nation, stimulated by the absence of foreign trade during the war, will have expanded to an extent never attained before. Suddenly peace is declared and immediately the country has to face keen competition from a rival state with a much more advanced industrial economy, supported by vast capital resources. The fiercer the onslaught of this competition, immediately after the cessation of hostilities, the greater will be the threat to the future prosperity of the whole industrial economy of the less advanced country. In these circumstances it is self evident that a nation, placed in peril in this way, will try to reverse the process and will endeavour to return to the situation that existed during the war. It will isolate itself as much as possible from its powerful rival. It will do this rather than indulge in rash fiscal experiments which might endanger the future prosperity of millions of its citizens. This is what happened in France at the time of the Restoration after the collapse of Napoleon's empire. The French government tried to introduce free trade, as far as this was possible, but very soon it was horrified at the disastrous consequences of this policy and it quickly returned to a policy of prohibitions.

An economist, with any pretensions to the wisdom of a statesman, who has grasped the true nature of industrial development must surely recognise that – in the situation that we have just described – an application of the theory of productive powers fully justifies the imposition of prohibitions. He cannot escape this conclusion whatever abstract economic theories he may once have advanced. At the end of the Napoleonic wars the first duty of the French government was to preserve the economy as it existed at that time. Industries had not developed sufficiently for the government to conclude that they were strong enough to survive and to expand without the aid of a tariff. Just as all industries had been protected during the war so all industries needed protection after the war. These safeguards were needed until experience had shown which industries could be permanently established and what degree of protection would be required to ensure their survival. At first all that was needed, in the interests of the whole economy, was to give every industry the chance to prove that it could survive. It was clearly the duty of the government, on grounds of public morality alone, to do this since – owing to the war and to its own policy – it had promoted the creation of new branches of manufacture. The government had persuaded people to risk their capital, their technical knowledge, their skills, and their future prosperity in the new industries. The establishment of these industries had certainly been of great advantage to the nation during the period of hostilities. The manufacturing enterprises had not only satisfied the requirements of the country but had also created a new market for agricultural products at a time when farmers could not sell their produce abroad. And the new industries have borne their share of taxation and have increased the ability of the country to defend itself. So it would have been not only the height of ingratitude on the part of the government but also an act of political folly to sacrifice those industries as soon as peace was declared. A nation which so abused the trust of its citizens would suffer for it in the event of another war. If hostilities broke out again the government could not hope to rely again upon the enterprise of men whose trust had been shamefully abused. It is the duty of a government – and it is to its own advantage – to retain the confidence of the citizens. Even those branches of manufacture which may eventually fail and may not be able to claim that permanent tariff protection for them is in the national interest, could argue that they were being unfairly treated if they were left to their fate – left to collapse completely – because unrestricted competition from abroad was allowed the moment peace was declared. Even those industries have a right to be treated with the greatest compassion. If the government decides that they cannot be saved from collapse it can at least postpone the evil day. The industry should be allowed to run down gradually so that factory owners and workers, whose livelihoods are at stake, can suffer as little as possible and can have an opportunity of entering some other industry. Immediately after a war a government cannot know which industries will never prosper and will never add to the wealth of the country. And a government cannot foresee the full extent of the damage that would be inflicted upon the national economy by the introduction of free trade. It cannot therefore decide what steps should be taken to alleviate the harm that would be caused by the introduction of free trade.

There are even weightier considerations which should be mentioned. During the Napoleonic wars France diverted most of her material and intellectual resources to her war effort. Little could be done to promote those aspects of national life which stimulate industrial production, such as technical education, roads, canals, and river shipping. Only when the wars were over could the state concentrate all its energies on stimulating the growth of manu-factures. Only then could vast human and material resources be brought together which had formerly been devoted to the war effort or which had been used by industry because they could not be used by the army. When the wars ended, both agriculture and industry could attract capital recently used for military purposes. Companies were formed to promote new manufacturing enterprises and steps were taken to improve transport facilities and to promote the expansion of the coal and iron industries. And in this period we find that representatives of agriculture and industry secured representation in the French legislature.

In wartime all contacts with foreign countries were interrupted since people could not travel or trade abroad. Only when the war ended could the raw materials and manufactured products that France required be purchased from abroad. Only then could the French resume their export trade in those manufactured articles in the production of which French craftsmen excelled. Who could then foresee the consequences for French industry of this resumption of international trade?

When peace was restored the French could travel to England and could judge for themselves what industrial progress had been made in that country in the last twenty years. They could see how this progress had been achieved. They were fired with the desire to introduce into France the new processes, the new machines, and the new advances in technology. Only when this had been achieved could France, under the shelter of her system of prohibitions, hope to attract foreign capital and skill to her shores.

What wise and sensible French statesman could at that time have contemplated giving up a fiscal system which, over a period of twenty years, had encouraged the growth of industries of all kinds? How could he think of doing such a thing at the very moment when the system of prohibitions was on the verge of achieving its greatest success? What fate would have been in store for France if her industries had been sacrificed to unrestricted competition from foreign goods? And what would be the position of France today if that had been allowed to happen?

Only those entirely lacking in practical experience – immediately the Napoleonic wars ended – have regarded the adoption of the prohibitive system as a pernicious policy. Certainly nothing worse could have happened to J. B. Say than to be appointed a minister of state on the day that Louis XVIII was restored to the throne.

Although the system of prohibitions was undoubtedly necessary and useful to France immediately after the Napoleonic wars, it does not follow that this fiscal policy will always be necessary and useful in the future. Although circumstances may make it imperative that the system of prohibitions should be established this system should be regarded as only a transitional policy. The government should endeavour to introduce a protective tariff as soon as possible. And the policy of tariff protection is only necessary and useful if it is regarded as a step on the road that eventually leads to the establishment of universal international free trade.

CHAPTER TWENTY THREE

Tariffs: the Policy of Protection

IT HAS BEEN seen that the system of prohibitions is a natural consequence of long wars which interrupt peaceful contacts between two great nations for many years. In the same way the policy of tariff protection is a result of shorter wars. It may also be brought about if a predominantly industrial state puts an end to a long established trade with an agricultural country by adopting a hostile tariff policy.

There are many ways in which tariffs can encourage the development of industries. Countries with different material and human resources and different economies will require different tariffs. One type of tariff will be suitable for a country which has previously had a prohibitive system while another type will be suitable for a country which is reorganising an existing protective tariff. One tariff will be suitable for a purely agricultural country, while another will be suitable for a country in which various branches of manufacture have already made some progress.

In order to explain how tariffs can be adapted to the requirements of particular countries we shall imagine a state which has – or can secure – a surplus of foodstuffs and raw materials such as wool and cotton. The social and moral condition of this country and its political institutions are suitable for industrial expansion. The country exports wool and cereals to an industrial state and imports manufactured goods from that state. Let us suppose that the industrialised country decides to impose high import duties on wool and grain. In such circumstances the agrarian country would be forced to retaliate by imposing import duties on manufactured goods from the industrialised state. The tariff policy of the agrarian country would be influenced by the level of wages earned by its workers. The government would have to consider if it would be necessary to offer higher wages in order to attract workers to industry at a time when there was still plenty of new land available for farming. In such circumstances a government should favour the establishment of industries which do not require a large labour force but can be started if cheap fuel and raw materials – and the necessary technical knowledge – are available. On the other hand if a country produces cheap foodstuffs and raw materials and the wages earned by its workers are low, the government should protect those industries which provide employment to a large number of workers.

No country should try to promote the immediate expansion of all branches of manufacture. At first – for the reasons that we have mentioned – it should attempt to stimulate only those industries which have an assured home market and appear to have the best chance of success.

Even these industries should not at first be protected by high import duties. Such duties would not increase the revenues of the state and would be oppressive as far as consumers are concerned. The best policy would be to start with moderate duties and to raise them by a predetermined sliding scale until they are high enough to assure the industry of a dominant position in the home market. On each occasion that the import duty is raised there will be an equivalent increase in the competition between manufacturers so that the price of the manufactured goods will progressively decline. When this happens the consumers will have no cause to complain of the import duties. As we explained in chapter 16 the expansion of a country's industrial power is accompanied by an improvement in the standard of living of its citizens. As soon as manufacturers have secured a dominant position in the home market, the import duty can be reduced on a sliding scale so that competition from foreign factories is gradually allowed. This competition, however, should be permitted to exist to only a limited extent. The appearance of foreign goods will stimulate competition between rival firms at home. Foreigners should be allowed no more than a fair share of the annual expansion in the demand for manufactured goods. Every nation which enjoys a harmonious balance between industry and agriculture enjoys also an annual increase in population and production, which automatically increases the demand for manufactured goods every year.

But if, for any reason, circumstances change, a government should reverse its policy. Suppose that foreigners succeeded in gaining more than their fair share of the increased demand. Suppose that they were actually able to supply all the increased demand and threatened to restore the situation that existed before the imposition of the tariff. This might happen because, for some reason, foreign manufacturers enjoyed a temporary advantage over home producers. Owing to a trade recession, for example, they might decide to get rid of their surplus goods at any price. If this happened the government should promptly restore higher import duties until the former position was re-established. A minister of state should be empowered to do this without waiting for the next meeting of the legislature.

These principles are undoubtedly valid particularly when fixing import duties on cloths made from cotton, wool, hemp, and flax since there is a huge internal demand for these products. A country with a large population employs at least a fifteenth or a tenth of its people in satisfying the demand of the home market for textiles. These industries stimulate agriculture by fostering an increased demand for foodstuffs and raw materials.

We have explained in chapter 17 that the imposition of import duties on textile raw materials, such as cotton, wool, hemp, and flax, will eventually fail to produce the desired effects. As we shall show in chapter 25 the only way to deal with this difficulty is to grant subsidies to home producers.

A country such as the United States which has had a high level of wages for a long time should not attempt to protect industries, such as the manufacture of silks, which rely upon artistic patterns and upon operatives who have considerable skill but are prepared to work for moderate wages. The success of the silk industry depends upon skills handed on from one generation of workers to the next. The United States should not protect a silk industry of its own so long as it can import silks in exchange for some of its own products. If an import duty were levied on silks it should be regarded as a revenue duty on the rich. Large imports of silks will not harm the productive powers of the nation. Indeed they will stimulate the production of the goods which are exported in exchange for silks.

Pig iron and coal are imports of considerable significance. It is desirable to consider very carefully if the natural resources of a country favour the opening up of coalmines or the establishment of ironworks. If conditions are unfavourable there is no point in levying import duties on coal or pig iron. The country should facilitate the importation of coal and pig iron since they are materials which are indispensable to the expansion of the economy.

But if the necessary natural resources are available, import duties should be imposed upon coal and pig iron, though they should not be so high as to reduce consumption. The best policy would be for the state to foster these industries by improving internal communications – canals and railways – as much as possible. And if there is not enough private capital available for the development of the mining industry the state should itself invest in joint stock mining companies and it should forego any dividend on its shares so long as private investors are not receiving any interest on their capital.

The principle that we have suggested for levying import duties on textiles should be reversed for iron goods. The less work that is done on iron goods in the manufacturing process the lower should be the duty levied on imports. The more that is done in the manufacturing process the greater should be the protection afforded to such products. Iron is a raw material that influences all the productive powers of a country. The less the work put into the manufacture of iron products the more damaging and dangerous are the consequences of making them more expensive.

An exception to this rule should be made in favour of plants making machines. If a country has industries sufficiently advanced to require large numbers of modern machines of various kinds but does not have the engineering workshops which make them, it would be foolish to impose high import duties on machinery. Such a policy would gravely endanger the future productive powers of the country. This argument is valid for a country which has just begun to establish import duties to protect its new industries. Here too, as with mining, the state would be well advised to foster the establishment of joint stock companies to set up model engineering workshops for the construction of machinery. If a war were to break out these workshops could be expanded and their output would meet all the country's requirements as far as machines were concerned. All newly invented machines should be allowed to enter the country for a certain period without payment of any import duty.

In general it may be observed that in fixing the rates of import duties to protect home industries it is important for a government to consider the level of prices and wages as well as the availability of capital and raw materials. The government should also assess the efficiency of the communications between its own country and the foreign countries with which it trades and with which it may have to compete.

117

CHAPTER TWENTY FOUR

Transition from the System of Prohibitions to the Policy of Protection

THE PRINCIPLES laid down in the last chapter are valid only when applied to a country which has just started to impose import duties to protect its industries. The position of a country which already safeguards its industries by prohibitions but proposes to change to the policy of protection is quite different. In view of the fundamental principles already discussed it is clear that a sound tariff should be instrumental in promoting the stability of the economy. Any sudden violent change in the rate of duties, however well-intentioned, would be most imprudent and contrary both to natural justice and to the welfare of society.

This applies even to import duties on raw materials and foodstuffs which are bad in themselves. If the state imposes these restrictions much capital and labour are attracted to a particular branch of production. It is contrary to common sense and to natural justice and it is contrary to the general welfare of the economy for a state suddenly to withdraw these restrictions since this would involve many people in grievous losses. Both capital and labour would be penalised with disastrous results. The removal of such import duties should take place in an orderly fashion. They should be reduced by annual instalments of a quarter or a third until only a small duty is levied. This duty should be regarded as a revenue duty payable by the foreigner, as an equivalent to taxes paid by home producers.

A different situation arises as far as manufactured goods are concerned. Before imposing import duties on manufactured goods the government of a country should undertake a thorough investigation to make sure that everything possible has been done to secure the maximum advantages from the system of prohibitions that can be achieved by an efficient and energetic administration.

Even if this is not done it is still desirable to announce in advance the date on which an import duty will be levied on particular manufactured goods, which were formerly prohibited from entering the country. It is only fair that interested parties should be given this information so that they can make preparations in view of the forthcoming change. The date should be fixed in plenty of time and in the intervening period – long or short – the government should do everything possible in its power to remove any obstacles that may be holding up the expansion of a particular branch of industry.

It is also necessary – in accordance with the principles suggested in the last chapter – to give advance notice of the sliding scale which is to replace prohibitions. The sliding scale should start with high import duties which should be reduced every year until they reach a level which still gives home industry adequate growth in demand for particular manufactured goods. At the same time, as we suggested in the last chapter, the administration should be given the necessary authority to increase import duties if, for any reasons, the country's manufacturers were suddenly to be threatened by foreign competition.

The following measures should be taken by an industrialised state in preparation for the transition from a system of prohibitions to a policy of protection.

1. The national transport system should be expanded to the fullest extent. This includes canals, railways, roads, steam shipping, and river shipping. Tolls should be fixed at a level that will stimulate industrial expansion in the hope that the costs of construction will eventually be covered. They should not be fixed at such a level as to raise immediately the funds necessary to pay investors interest on the capital invested in these public works.

2. The government should foster the extension of technical education to the best of its ability. Technical and agricultural schools and colleges should be established not only in the capital of a country but throughout the provinces. The cost of building these schools should be defrayed by the provincial authorities. They should be run under the supervision of provincial chambers of commerce and agriculture and competition between them should be encouraged. The Ministry of Education should exercise only a general oversight over technical and agricultural schools.

3. Restrictions upon the entry of raw materials and foodstuffs into a country should, as far as possible, be reduced or removed.

4. Every year the government should hold an industrial exhibition in which the best foreign products and the best products made in a country should be shown side by side – with prices indicated.

119

5. If a government observes that manufacturers are producing goods lower in quality and higher in price than those made abroad and if it is satisfied that this is the fault of the local industrialists it should offer substantial prizes as a reward to those manufacturers who, within a specified period, are able to make goods which approach those made abroad in quality and price. The ability to manufacture such goods regularly should also be considered when awarding prizes. Acceptance of such an award should be conditional upon a firm allowing workers employed elsewhere to visit its factory so as to improve their technical knowledge.

6. Should a government decide that manufacturers have failed to make products which are as good as those made abroad simply because they have not been able to secure the services of a sufficient number of hardworking skilled men it should offer prizes to workers who reach a high standard of technical skill. It should also offer prizes to firms which, in a particular period, have succeeded in attracting foreign workers of proven skill and reliability into their employment.

7. A government should make an annual investigation so as to establish which firms fail to reach satisfactory standards of production and the results of the enquiry should be made public.

8. The Minister of Commerce should regularly send large numbers of experts in economics, in public administration, and in various branches of manufacture to foreign countries in order to investigate particular industries or particular aspects of agriculture. The experts should submit reports on their investigations and should explain how their observations can benefit the development of industries in their own country. These reports should be published annually as an encouragement to the experts themselves and as a method of informing the public about economic developments in foreign countries. Experts who do good work and who show outstanding ability in the performance of their duties should be appointed to consular posts abroad or to posts in the Ministry of Finance or other branches of the civil service.

9. It is essential that the workers of a country which is becoming industrialised should be well paid and well fed. It is therefore necessary that the absolute necessities of life should be taxed either very lightly or not at all. The worst imposts – taxes which are contrary to natural law – are *octrois* (consumption duties) levied upon the commonest foodstuffs, fuel, soap, meat, and ordinary wine

and beer.[1] No worker can be expected to increase his output if he is not getting sufficient nourishment. Roast beef and porter have done more for the greatness of England than one might suppose. All English parliamentary enquiries prove that the output of the English worker is two or three times as great as that of workers in other countries. The influence of the earnings of workers upon the prices of manufactured goods should not be judged by the existence of a high or a low level of wages. It should be judged by the relation between wages and output. If workers are poorly nourished their children will be stunted and weakly and so the productive powers of future generations will be destroyed. Moreover it is unjust to place the same heavy indirect taxes upon those who can afford only the barest necessities of life and those who are able to live in the lap of luxury. The worst tax of all is that upon salt because it directly threatens a nation's productive powers.

It would be injudicious to make these proposals without also suggesting how to meet the deficit in the national budget which would follow the abolition of all taxes on the necessities of life. An income tax would bridge the gap. No one has yet put forward a reasonable and sensible objection to the introduction of income tax. Its opponents have been content to argue that there are insuperable practical difficulties in assessing and collecting such a tax. This is true enough in a despotic state but it is not true in a constitutional state. In a democratic society the administration operates with the support of sound institutions and patriotic sentiments. If each citizen made a declaration of his income – and if this was checked by three different juries – a satisfactory assessment could be made and nobody would have cause to complain about it.

It is particularly important that *octrois* should be abolished and that the lost revenue should be made good by imposing an income tax. The removal of these consumption duties would help to reduce the cost of manufactured goods and would be most beneficial to the workers.

10. A government should do everything in its power to increase the currency in circulation to keep pace with the growth of industry. It should also promote the establishment of public credit institutions. It should encourage the establishment of provincial banks all over the country and these banks should be authorised to issue their

1. [List's note] See Charles Dupin, *Forces productives et commerciales de la France* (2 vols., Paris, 1827), pp. 61-73.

own notes.[1] But great care should be taken to ensure that these banks were run on sound financial principles.

National banks in the capital of a country, which have no branches in the provinces and issue notes only in large denominations, cannot adequately carry out the functions of country banks or cannot carry them out at all.

11. The government should try to foster the founding of new companies but should endeavour to prevent any misuse of this form of business organisation. It should forbid the issue of bearer bonds and should make provision for the public inspection of the working of all companies.

CHAPTER TWENTY FIVE

Transition from the Policy of Protection to the Policy of as much Free Trade as possible

WE REGARD ourselves as citizens of the world, but our faith in humanity rests upon the solid basis of nationalism. We can certainly envisage a situation in which a country would find freedom of trade preferable to a restrictive fiscal policy. We are citizens of a nation before we are citizens of the world. We devote our faculties to the energetic pursuit of the culture, welfare, fame, and security of the nation to which we belong. We strive towards the same goal for humanity. But the fortunes of humanity must be compatible with the fortunes of our country. We cannot support any policy that would harm our country in order to benefit the whole world. This is because we owe to our country our culture, our language, our livelihood, and our intellectual values. Nature has implanted in our hearts the desire that future generations should enjoy the same benefits from the nation as we enjoy today.

A time comes when certain countries and regions are capable of

1. [In the same year that he wrote *The Natural System of Political Economy* List submitted a memorandum to Louis Philippe recommending the establishment of joint stock banks to finance the construction of railways (F. List, *Werke*, Vol. V, pp. 95-8).]

adopting a policy of free trade instead of a policy of protection. We propose, however, that such countries should retain those import duties which are necessary to compensate manufacturers for the burden of taxation that they are expected to bear. The countries we have in mind are:

1. All purely agrarian countries which – for reasons given in chapter 10 – are not yet capable of developing industries even with the aid of a tariff. By trading freely with industrialised states these agrarian countries can more quickly develop their economies.

2. All colonies, all primitive regions, and all backward barbarous regions.

3. The leading industrial state in the world, because the high quality and the low prices of its manufactured products enables it to dominate the home market and to compete successfully in foreign markets.

4. Those industrialised states of the second rank which consider that they are strong enough to compete with the leading manufacturing country.

5. All countries in the world as far as commerce in raw materials and foodstuffs is concerned.

In this transition period, as in previous transition periods, a government should work out and announce in plenty of time a definite sliding scale for the reduction of import duties. It should also be prepared if necessary to impose import duties again if foreign competition should at any time threaten the nation's industrial forces.

In this connection the following observations may be made:

Import duties levied purely for revenue purposes should never be levied at so high a rate as to lead to a perceptible decline in consumption.

Export subsidies are a miserable palliative which cannot remedy the injurious effects of pernicious import duties on raw materials. Export subsidies direct to foreign countries capital and industry which might be much more usefully employed at home. Since they encourage fraud they are, from a financial point of view, harmful to the state. Finally export subsidies are not only useless and unnecessary but they force other countries to retaliate and to introduce such subsidies themselves.

Restrictions on the export of raw materials, foodstuffs, or manufactured goods cannot be justified by logical arguments or on economic grounds. Only in time of war can such restrictions be justified.

A country may derive real permanent advantages from companies trading abroad, even though they sometimes fail to show a profit for their shareholders. This occurs when a country has highly developed industries and agriculture but has so far made little progress with regard to foreign trade. Alternatively such a country may have lost its foreign commerce as the result of a long war. In such circumstances companies trading abroad are able to inspire – or to revive – a spirit of enterprise and they can secure for a country valuable information concerning foreign markets. But these companies do more harm than good in a country which has not made much progress in establishing industries or in a country which has already developed a considerable foreign trade.

CHAPTER TWENTY SIX

How best to introduce and to foster Free Trade

J. B. SAY has inspired economists with such a horror of commercial treaties that we would not presume to raise a voice in favour of such agreements unless we were able to explain the reasons for Say's views and to show the weakness of his arguments. In fact Say is thinking only of agreements similar to the Methuen Treaty.[1] Such treaties have always been found to have thoroughly unsatisfactory results and these results have been the exact opposite of those which Say declares follow the adoption of Free Trade. It is therefore easy to understand Say's opposition to every kind of commercial treaty. He considered that all such treaties were useless because the results of those concluded so far were inconsistent with his economic

1. [By the Methuen (Anglo-Portuguese) commercial treaty of 1703 Portugal removed her prohibition on the import of woollen cloth from England while England agreed always to admit Portuguese wines at two-thirds of the duty imposed upon French wines. See chapter 27 below.]

doctrines. Say's theory is of great value – except that it has no practical application.

There are only two ways by which Free Trade can be introduced. The first is to set up a world state like the European empire that Napoleon tried to establish. The second is for countries to conclude commercial treaties. Care must of course be taken not to conclude treaties by which one nation enjoys the oysters while another has to be content with the shells. Commercial treaties must give equal advantages to all the countries which sign them. All countries must secure guarantees for the future survival and prosperity of their industries.

France and the United States are two countries which would benefit greatly from the conclusion of a commercial treaty.[1] It is very important for France to maintain her market for silks in the United States because the population and economic growth of that country are accelerating at such a pace that the demand for silks will double, or more than double, every ten years. There is an enormous potential demand for French silks in the United States. On the other hand so long as wages are so high in the United States that country will not be interested in establishing a silk industry of its own. This branch of manufacture takes a long time to develop and requires the services of skilled operatives who are satisfied with moderate wages. It is to the advantage of the Americans to buy silks from abroad, in exchange for goods that they can produce, rather than to attempt to manufacture silks at home. Again it is to the advantage of the Americans – particularly those living in New England, the Middle States, and the West – that France should accept in return for her silks not only cotton, tobacco, and potash but also all kinds of farm produce. Unfortunately France imposes very high import duties on cotton and potash without thereby

1. [List had long been interested in promoting trade between France and the United States. In 1827 in his *Outlines of American Political Economy* he had written that France will "ever be a good and sure market for American cotton". "There are strong reasons to believe that France would readily increase the importation of other products from the United States, particularly tobacco, ham, lard, and tallow, if the United States would take proper measures to increase their importation from France" (reprinted in F. List, *Werke*, Vol. II, p. 154). In 1830 List had undertaken a mission to Paris in the hope of persuading the French government to enter into commercial negotiations with the United States. See also F. List, "Idées sur les réformes économiques, commerciales et financières, applicables à la France" in the *Revue Encyclopédique*, March and November 1831 (reprinted in F. List, *Werke*, Vol. V, pp. 59-91).]

conferring any benefits on the French people. And France has a tobacco monopoly which greatly limits the consumption of tobacco.

It is evident that France and the United States would both benefit from a reduction in the onerous French import duties on cotton and potash. This would be in accordance with the doctrine that we advanced in chapter [25?]. And if the French tobacco monopoly were replaced by an import duty this would almost entirely compensate the state for the loss of revenue raised from the monopoly. But such changes could hardly be brought about except by the conclusion of a commercial treaty. It would be easy to conclude a series of other similar trade agreements which would be highly advantageous to the countries concerned.

To pave the way for the conclusion of advantageous commercial treaties a world trade congress should be convened at which all countries should be represented by experienced and well qualified experts. Such a congress should consider how the common interests of the various nations can best be served and how opposing interests could be reconciled. The congress should consider the varied interests of regions and societies at different stages of economic development – such as industrialised, agrarian, colonial, and primitive societies. It should examine the needs of countries which have reached the second or the third stage of industrial development in relation to the world's leading manufacturing country. It should consider the economic relations between two particular countries and between certain groups of countries. The deliberations of the congress would provide information to people all over the world concerning economic problems. This would encourage governments and legislative assemblies to adopt measures which would be to the advantage of all countries and it would enable governments to enlighten the citizens of all states on these matters. It would, for example, be much easier for the British government to secure acceptance of the repeal of the Corn Laws if this measure were to follow discussions at a world trade congress. The discussions at the congress should cover all the matters mentioned in chapter 17. These are topics which are of interest to all countries. The deliberations of the congress would throw light on the following topics – the advantages of universal free trade in raw materials and agricultural products; the advantages to be secured by all industrialised countries by agreeing to the imposition of uniform import duties on manufactured goods; the advantages of establishing common measures to secure universal peace, public order, and security of persons and property. Above all a world trade congress would facilitate the establishment of the freedom of the seas since it would give the lesser mercantile countries an opportunity to appreciate their real interest in this matter.

In chapters 7 and 8 we dealt with this aspect of the problem. We suggested that France and the United States should, in their own interests, take the lead in calling a world trade congress. There are reasons to believe that a suggestion of this kind would be supported by all the countries on the Continent. If these countries collaborated it can hardly be doubted that England, too, would send representatives to the proposed world trade congress, if only to keep abreast with what was happening. In chapter 7 we showed how powerful are the reasons which might make England decide to adopt a liberal commercial policy. Here we may add that England's cotton mills have now become very dependent upon the United States for their supplies of raw cotton.

The author considers that the explanatory memorandum attached to the question posed by the Academy[1] justifies him in putting forward his proposal for the holding of a world trade congress although this is admittedly a somewhat daring suggestion.

He hopes that he has paid proper attention to all the points raised in the Academy's memorandum:

"Will it be possible to establish Free Trade in wartime as well as in peacetime by an international treaty which – however incomplete – could still be regarded as a great step forward in the progress of humanity?"

The great principle of "free ships, free goods" has already been enunciated by Catherine the Great of Russia and by George Washington. But so far it has not been possible to secure the universal acceptance of this principle. It is obvious – proof is hardly required – that the universal acceptance and strict observation of this principle of international law would remove most of the disastrous consequences that war brings to all branches of industry. The author can see no way of achieving this aim unless the proposed doctrine of international law is universally accepted.

1. [List's note] See Charles Dupin, "Sur le prix d'économie politique relatif aux moyens d'établir la liberté commerciale (December 28, 1836), [Reprinted in F. List, *Werke (Schriften, Reden, Briefe)* Vol. IV: *Das natürliche System der politischen Ökonomie*, 1837 (1971), pp. 39-44]

If, however, there came a time when the maritime powers of the second and third rank were in a position to force England to accept the doctrine of "free ships, free goods" it could be done only if they collaborated closely. The best way to secure this co-operation would be through a world trade congress, as we have already proposed. Such a conference would be the simplest way of showing the nations on the Continent where their common interests lay. Even if the nineteenth century should pass without the doctrine "free ships, free goods" being generally accepted, the twentieth century will surely see its adoption.

When that time comes England will be the country to advocate the adoption of the principle and people will discuss how best to check the arbitrary power of the United States of America.

CHAPTER TWENTY SEVEN

History of England's Economic Policy

ADAM SMITH and his disciples have repeatedly asserted that England's commercial policy has not been responsible for her present prosperity. They argue that England became prosperous in spite of her commercial policy. Our own arguments would fall to the ground if this were true. We believe that we can reveal Adam Smith's errors. We consider that Adam Smith's biographer was right in complaining that this profound thinker was prone to make paradoxical assertions.

Before the twelfth century England was a very poor and primitive agricultural country. Then the significance of her flocks of sheep – the foundation of her future prosperity – was increased by trade with the Hansa merchants who began to import manufactured goods from Germany, Flanders, the Mediterranean countries and the East. In exchange the Hansa merchants exported from England butter, lead, tin and particularly wool which was sent in large quantities to Germany and Flanders where it was spun and woven. Then some of the cloth was sent back to England.

By the thirteenth century the export of wool – a thousand bales a year – had already given English agriculture its first stimulus. But in Edward III's reign the government realised that England could do better than to export wool in order to import cloth. Edward III invited weavers from Flanders and Brabant to settle in England.[1] Political unrest in their own countries led them to accept the invitation. At the same time Edward III forbade his subjects to wear any garments other than those made from English cloth.[2]

Following in the footsteps of his predecessors, Edward IV ordered foreign merchants to export English cloth to the value of the goods that they brought into England. In 1463 he actually prohibited the import of all foreign cloths as well as many other products.[3]

The Hansa towns by force of arms secured the repeal of this statute by the Treaty of Utrecht in 1474 but the manufacture of cloth was so firmly established in England that fifty years later Henry VII was able to revive the statute. Once more foreign merchants had to export English manufactured goods of equal value to the goods which they brought to England from abroad.

In Henry VIII's reign most of the descendants of the foreign artisans had raised the prices of all the necessities of life. Instead of regarding this as a beneficial consequence of the activities of the artisans the King criticised them for placing the country in danger of famine. He ordered 15,000 of them to be expelled and he encouraged the Hansa merchants to increase their imports by restoring their former privileges. This policy was greatly to the disadvantage of the English artisans. But the former commercial policy was revived first in Edward VI's reign and then – even more vigorously – in the reign of Queen Elizabeth when English artisans

1. [List's note] Rymer, *Foedera*, p. 496, De Witt, p. 45 [List's reference to Rymer appears to have been taken from David Hume, *The History of England* (12 vols, 1789), Vol. II, p. 523 *et. seq.* and the reference to De Witt from Adam Anderson, *An Historical and Chronological Deduction of the Origin of Commerce* (6 vols, Dublin, 1790), Vol. I, p. 402 *et. seq.*]
2. [List's note] 2 Edward III, Cap V [i.e. 1328]
3. [List's note] 3 Edward IV, Cap IV [List quoted the preamble to this statute in a footnote to *The National System of Political Economy*, 1841 (edition of 1966, p. 17).]

not only gained control over the home market for their ordinary rough cloths but were also able to export 200,000 pieces of cloth to Germany and the Low Countries every year.

In James I's reign it was estimated that the value of England's cloth exports had reached the enormous total of £2,000,000 a year. This represented nine tenths of all England's exports. At that time English cloth – manufactured from the home clip – was prized and welcomed in the chief markets of Europe. The expansion of the production of wool and the growth in the number of spinners and weavers led to a remarkable increase in the incomes of the land-owners who were now prepared to promote the progress and pros-perity of the cloth industry. But in other countries at this time the nobles had not yet begun to appreciate how the growth of industry could promote the expansion of agriculture. In James I's reign English cloths exported to the Continent were still finished and dyed in Flanders. The government, however, promoted the establishment of the finishing process in England – as well as the manufacture of fine high quality cloths – by prohibitions and by other measures.

By the beginning of the eighteenth century England dominated the markets of Europe in what was then the most important branch of industry. In 1703 the signing of the famous Methuen Treaty enabled England to secure for herself a dominant trading position in the Portuguese colonies. From time immemorial Portugal had possessed a breed of sheep which produced wool of the very highest quality. In ancient times Strabo reported that, even before his day, a fine breed of ewes had been sent to Portugal at a cost of one talent each. From these ewes great flocks of sheep developed so that Portugal was able to produce large quantities of fine wool for export.

In 1687 the Portuguese minister d'Ericeira decided to encourage the immigration of foreign manufacturers and artisans and to forbid the import of cloth from abroad. In this way he hoped to supply both the home and the colonial markets with cloth made in Portugal. This policy was pursued with great success between 1687 and 1703.

After the death of Count d'Ericeira the English ambassador in Lisbon – John Methuen – persuaded the King and the grandees that it would be greatly to their advantage if Portugal were to sell wool and wine to England in return for cloth. In 1703 a commercial treaty was concluded which provided for a reduction in the English import duty on Portuguese wine to one third of that levied on wine imported from any other country. This gave Portugal a secure market for her wine. In return Portugal fixed her import duty on English cloth at 23 per cent.

To what extent did this treaty fulfil the hopes of the King and the grandees of Portugal? English writers provide the answer to this question. Before long the goods sent from England to Portugal were valued at £1,000 more than the Portuguese products sent to England. The editor of *The British Merchant*, when dedicating [the third volume of] his book to Sir Paul Methuen, the son of the English ambassador to Portugal, wrote: "We gain a greater balance of trade from Portugal than from any other country. Since the treaty came into force our exports to that country have risen from £300,000 to £1,500,000".[1] In the same volume it was stated that the balance of trade was so much in England's favour that the Portuguese currency was devalued by 12 per cent in English markets, which was very much to Portugal's disadvantage. English merchants evaded the provisions of the Methuen Treaty by making false declarations concerning the value of the cloth that they sent to Portugal. The value that they declared was only one half of the real value. In this way they made certain that the import duty of 23 per cent would afford no protection to the Portuguese artisans. The result was that the Portuguese cloth industry collapsed.[2] *The British Merchant* declared with admirable frankness that by this advantageous treaty "we brought away so much of their silver as to leave them very little for their necessary occasions, and then we began to bring away their gold".[3]

Anderson, who reports these facts, adds with charming naiveté: "The most just and beneficial convention has remained inviolable to this day; which has preserved an uninterrupted friendship and alliance between both nations. And may it ever continue".[4] We

1. [The dedication was as follows: "Your father, often Ambassador Extraordinary to the King of Portugal, procured for Great Britain that glorious Treaty of Commerce by which She gains above a Million a year. By this Treaty we paid our Armies in Spain and Portugal and drew from thence, in the late War, considerable Sums for our Troops in other Parts, without remitting one Farthing from England; and at the same time coin'd in the Tower, above a Million of Portugal Gold in three Years" (*The British Merchant*, Vol. III, p. 11).]
2. [List's note] *The British Merchant*, Vol. III, p. 91.
3. [List's note] *The British Merchant*, Vol. III, p. 15.
4. [Adam Anderson, *An Historical and Chronological Deduction of the Origin of Commerce* (6 vols, Dublin 1790). Vol. III, p. 227 *et. seq.*]

invite the reader to note the price of an English alliance and English friendship!

We shall see later that the great Adam Smith does not accept the favourable judgment passed upon this treaty by English statesmen, merchants, and manufacturers. He regards the treaty as disadvantageous to England and advantageous to Portugal. Perhaps an examination of his arguments will reveal his weakness for paradoxes.

The facts that we have given show that the manufacture of woollen cloth was England's first and greatest industry. They show that ever since the thirteenth century England has first established and then fostered and preserved this industry by giving her artisans a monopoly of the home market and by opening up foreign markets for them by commercial treaties.

England has not always followed so enlightened a policy as far as trade in cereals is concerned. For centuries the government fixed the prices of foodstuffs and the wages of labourers. Before Elizabeth's reign the export of grain was prohibited. Indeed before the reign of Henry IV it was actually forbidden to move grain from one county to another.[1] Henry IV was the first monarch to grant licences which permitted such movement of grain. At various times regulations were actually made stating the number of sheep which each landowner could raise on his estate because the government feared that there would be a shortage of grain if the flocks of sheep were too large. Queen Elizabeth, on the other hand, allowed grain to be exported while James I actually found this trade to be so advantageous that he encouraged it by the payment of subsidies.

The growth of England's overseas commerce and shipping has been promoted in the same way as the expansion of her agriculture and industry, namely by restrictive regulations.

Henry VIII was dependent upon the loan of ships from the Hanseatic League to maintain his navy. At this time the expansion of the cloth industry and the growth of towns increased the demand for coal.[2] The mineowners opened up new collieries and were able

1. [List's note] Hume, ch. 18 [i.e. David Hume, *The History of England*].
2. [List's note] The supremacy of Dutch shipping was originally based upon her fisheries as well as upon Peter Beukel's discovery of a method of salting herrings. The supremacy of English shipping, on the other hand, was originally based upon the coal trade and upon an Act of Parliament. In 1400 the nobles and citizens of London petitioned Henry IV to prohibit the use of sea coal because this was an injurious and unhealthy fuel. It was called sea coal because it was extracted from mines lying under

– in addition to supplying the home market – to export large quantities of coal. This led to a remarkable expansion of coastal and overseas shipping. In the middle of the seventeenth century some 900 ships used the harbour of Newcastle-upon-Tyne – 600 in Dutch hands – and all were employed in the coal trade. The development of shipping led to the growth of a shipbuilding industry and to a considerable expansion in the number of sailors serving in the navy and the mercantile marine.[1] The English came to recognise that the time had come when shipping and shipbuilding – so important for the commerce and defence of a nation – should become independent of foreign influences.

For this reason the Rump Parliament passed the famous Navigation Act in 1651, which provided that foreign manufactured and agricultural products could be brought to England only in English ships. The captain had to be a native-born Englishman and three quarters of the crew had to be English. Foreign ships were allowed to bring to England only the produce of the country to which the ships belonged. The same law stated that only fish caught by English fishermen might be landed in English or Irish ports. Only English ships could carry fish out of these ports or from one English harbour to another.

As those responsible for the Act had intended the Navigation Act struck a fatal blow at Dutch naval supremacy and at the Dutch fishing industry. So seriously did the Dutch suffer that they immediately declared war upon England. On February 13, 1653 a great sea battle was fought and the Dutch were completely defeated. The result was that Dutch trade through the Straits of Dover was cut off while Dutch trade to the Baltic was seriously interrupted by English privateers. Dutch fishing was entirely suspended and 1,600 Dutch ships fell into English hands.[2] In his book on the public revenue

---

the sea bed. The citizens of London could hardly have realised that they were demanding the destruction of a trade that would one day be the foundation of England's sea power. For many years Newcastle-upon-Tyne has been a flourishing city because of the coal trade. Most of this commerce has been an export trade because for a long time the expansion of the consumption of coal in England itself was delayed by popular prejudice against this fuel. But as the population of the country increased – owing to the expansion of the manufacture of cloth – this prejudice against the use of coal vanished. [Willem Beukel invented a new method of gutting, salting, and curing fish. He died in 1397. Charles V erected a statue to him in Amsterdam.]

1. [List's note] Anderson, Vol. II, p. 511.
2. [List's note] Hume, Vol. V. p. 39.

Davenant[1] states that after the Dutch war the English mercantile marine was doubled in 28 years.[2]

Adam Smith is mistaken in supposing that the Navigation Act was passed because of national rivalries. The Act was based upon the maritime code of the Hanseatic towns. These cities had, in their turn, taken over the rules and regulations of Venice.[3] England therefore followed the example of two sea-going commercial powers and took advantage of several centuries of practical experience in these matters. Deliberately or involuntarily Adam Smith forgets to mention two earlier attempts – before the law passed by the Long Parliament – to introduce a navigation code. The first was in Henry VI's reign in 1461 when a proposal submitted by Parliament was rejected by the King.[4] The second was in 1622 in James I's reign when Parliament refused to accept a proposal for a navigation code made by the government.[5]

To such an extent does a navigation code partake of the very nature of a nation which realises that it is destined one day to become a great sea power that the United States had hardly finished fighting for its independence than Congress passed a restrictive law which aimed at promoting shipping and overseas commerce. This measure was even more successful in achieving its object than the English Navigation Act had been.

From the reign of Queen Elizabeth to the present day England has evolved a comprehensive method of encouraging industry. The

1. [Charles d'Avenant, *Discourses of the Public Revenues and on the Trade of England* (London, 1698: new edition in 5 volumes, 1771), Vol. I, p. 363.]

2. [List's note] Anderson reports (Vol. II, p. 552) that in England many responsible people considered the Navigation Act to be unjust and unworkable. They doubtless employed just as profound arguments in support of their views as those put forward by Say when he denounces the subsidies paid by the French government to promote the fishing industry and the mercantile marine. There were those who argued that the restrictions [imposed by the Navigation Act] were senseless and would have dreadful results, such as war, famine, and the destruction of England's trade. The Dutch, for their part, learned from bitter experience that they would have been well advised to share their trade with the English rather than to suffer such great losses and so ignominious a defeat. They attributed their downfall particularly to the fact that the English had bigger ships. Attention had often been drawn to this fact though it had never been considered to be of great importance. This point is of some interest if one compares English and American shipping. Every English naval officer visiting the United States is astonished at the size of American naval and merchant ships and warns his countrymen of disasters to come if the English government should fail to follow the example of the Americans with regard to shipbuilding.

3. [List's note] Anderson, *History of Commerce,* Vol. II, p. 46

4. [List's note] *Hume*, ch. 21.

5. [List's note] *Hume*, Vol. IV, p. 330.

government has prohibited imports from abroad and has fostered industry at home. Having closed their harbours to the Hanseatic merchants the English did everything in their power to persuade foreign artisans who were being persecuted to settle in England. By granting asylum to refugees from France and the Low Countries England attracted many new industries to her shores. The English government also signed commercial treaties with Russia, Turkey, and the Hanseatic League and granted privileges to chartered companies to trade in these countries and in the East Indies.[1]

Every nation has a particular industry in which it has led the world. Holland dyes vermilion cloths, Venice makes glassware, Germany manufactures iron and steel, France and Switzerland produce silks and watches, while fishermen from the Bay of Biscay are engaged in hunting whales.[2] Craftsmen have actually been sent to Persia to learn the art of making and dyeing carpets. And manu-

1. [List's note] Adam Smith and David Hume criticise Elizabeth for granting privileges of this kind to companies of merchants. They fail to appreciate that in those days the Hanseatic merchants were still strong and rich and that the Dutch were at the height of their power. If Elizabeth had acted according to the doctrines of these two scholars it is possible that the English would never have chased these foreigners out of their home market. This could be achieved only if the government supported companies of merchants and signed commercial treaties with foreign states.

At that time no English merchant was capable of opening up overseas commerce in competition with Hanseatic and Dutch merchants. On the other hand a chartered company – endowed with privileges and supported by commercial treaties and the strength of the navy – could summon up courage to trade overseas and could attract commercial capital from German and Dutch towns. Merchants from Hamburg and Lübeck, for example, lacking profits from their enterprises in foreign markets, went to England to enjoy the advantage of the trading privileges granted by the government.

If these trading companies made no profits at first it was not really a loss as far as the state was concerned. It should be regarded as an unavoidable sacrifice, without which England could never have built up the extensive overseas trade that she enjoys today. If England's industry later expanded when the privileges of the trading companies were withdrawn, it does not mean that the country would have prospered just as much, had the privileges not been enjoyed in the past. When the privileges were withdrawn England's commerce had long been firmly established and – by taking part in the joint enterprises of great chartered companies – individual merchants had gained a thorough knowledge of this type of trading. They now had the means and the initiative to pursue their ventures further afield. All industries are in the same position since early losses pave the way for later profits. Many inventors who enrich millions of people by their discoveries have lost their own capital while making their experiments. Privileges granted to chartered companies are like patents granted to inventors. Each is valuable for a certain period but when that period has elapsed the removal of both trading privileges and patents benefits society as a whole.

2. [List's note] Anderson, Vol. I, p. 127 and Vol. II, p. 350.

facturers have had a strong urge to master new techniques simply because they have enjoyed the support of a secure home market.

In England one of the most important laws ever passed was aimed at stimulating the fishing industry, that wonderful school for the training of sailors. Subsidies were granted which were based upon the tonnage of the fishing vessels and the size of the catch.

Of course it must be appreciated that other factors have also contributed to England's rise to the position of the leading commercial, maritime, and industrial country in the world. They include England's natural resources, the energetic character of the people, the geographical location of the country, and the uninterrupted development of political freedom – above all as a result of the revolution of 1689. Nevertheless it cannot be denied that England would never have reached her present dominant position without the continued protection given by the state first to the manufacture of woollens, then to the shipping and fishing industries, and finally to all branches of manufacture.

History teaches us that nations – like clever and fortunate individuals – frequently owe their success as much to the errors, follies, and ill-fortune of others as to their own exertions. We have already seen – and we shall see again in later chapters – how England has turned to her own advantage the decline and fall of the Hanseatic League, Flanders, Venice, Genoa, Spain, Portugal, France and Germany – a decline that was due sometimes to religious bigotry, sometimes to the privileges of the nobles, and sometimes to the oppression of despotic rulers. We shall show how England alone has been able, over the centuries, to use to her own advantage nearly all the fruits of the Reformation, the discovery of America, the opening up of a new route to India by way of the Cape of Good Hope, and the invention of printing and of gunpowder. But one must admit that England has shown herself worthy of benefitting from this wonderful inheritance by her own striking inventions and improvements which have given a new value to discoveries that have taken place elsewhere.

England gave the civilised world the first complete national network of highways and canals and so showed how truly remarkable are the results of constructing an efficient transport system. Such a system of communications vigorously stimulates all the productive powers of the nation. England showed the world how great was the wealth that could be derived from her coalmines and steelworks. England has produced new sources of energy, new machines, and new manufacturing processes which have greatly increased the efficiency of transport facilities and the output of labour.

By increasing her productive powers in this way England was able, by her own efforts, not merely to resist the terrible power of Napoleon for many years but finally to defeat him. England was far from being weakened by the long and bitter struggle which she had waged against the French. She actually emerged from the war stronger than before. This was because her productive powers had increased since she had been able to isolate the colonies of European countries in America, Africa, and Asia and to open them up as new markets for her manufactured goods. At the same time she seized the opportunity to extend her colonial possessions. Finally her victory over Napoleon enabled England to subjugate the whole world by her industrial power. She became a land of factories and warehouses. She developed into a sort of metropolis which treated the whole world as if it were a mere English province.

When peace was restored people all over the world fell under the spell of the theoretical economists, who argued that the doctrine of free trade should now be put into practice. Governments appeared to be willing to listen to these arguments. Russia, Scandinavia, Germany, Italy, Spain, Portugal and the United States seemed to be ready to accept English manufactured goods in exchange for their own products. Only France remained faithful to the policy of protection but even France might have made some concessions if England had opened her ports to French wines, brandies, and silks – though the total value of these products was much smaller than that of England's cotton piece goods, woollens, and iron products. Perhaps this was the time when England should have given up the policy of protection. As far as the Navigation Act was concerned she might have taken the advice given by Joseph Priestley many years before when he declared that "the time may come in which it will be as politic to repeal this Act as it was to make it".[1]

It would be difficult to imagine the degree of prosperity that the English would have achieved if they had continued to accept foreign products in exchange for their manufactured goods. Neither the states on the Continent – with the possible exception of France – nor the United States would have attempted to challenge Great

1. [List's note] Priestley, *Lectures on History and General Policy*, Part II, p. 289.

Britain's superiority. England would have imported the surplus produce of the vast regions opened up – and to be opened up in the future – in the United States. The millions of people in the new world – and the hundreds of millions who will be living there a century from today – would be wearing garments made from English cloth. Everything would have contributed to England's power and wealth. In such circumstances it is doubtful if the Russians or the Americans would ever have adopted the policy of protection. There would have been no German customs union. It would have been contrary to the interests of all the inhabitants of the agricultural countries to sacrifice immediate advantages today in the hope of gaining other advantages tomorrow. But, as a great poet once wrote, it is ordained that trees shall not grow into the sky. We have it on biblical authority that if providence proposes to humble a nation it first provides it with stupid rulers.

The policy pursued by Lord Castlereagh at home and abroad failed to secure for England the fruits of her victory. It placed the future prosperity of the country at the mercy of the aristocracy who promptly killed the goose which laid the golden eggs. Had the noble landowners accepted the fact that Great Britain was destined to be the industrial metropolis of the world they would have turned much of their land into vegetable gardens, pleasure gardens and meadows. They would have produced only those farm products which could not be imported. In this way they would have been able to charge tenant farmers much higher rents than they charged farmers who had been encouraged (by the Corn Laws) to grow cereals. But this will happen only at some time in the future and aristocrats are not renowned for their ability to look ahead. The great landowners preferred to raise rents immediately by reducing imports of foreign agricultural products by the imposition of prohibitions and high import duties. They forced the nations of the world to seek prosperity by following a different path from that indicated by the doctrine of free trade.

By the time that Canning and Huskisson were in office the great landowners had tasted too much of the forbidden fruit to be prepared to give it up – even if these statesmen had really intended to deprive them of it. Once a country has adopted the policy of protection it cannot accept a sudden change in the fiscal system even if it realises that the administration of the most powerful, the wealthiest, and the most industrialised nation in the world has passed into the hands of men who accept the doctrine of free trade. It would be the height of folly – dangerous stupidity – if those responsible for running a country should waver from the principles of their existing fiscal policy in return for empty words and promises. Those who make such promises are in no position to keep them. Even if the promises can be kept at the moment, no politician can give an absolutely firm guarantee that the fiscal policy which he has introduced will survive his departure from office.

Speeches in Parliament and articles in the press announced to an astonished world that the English cabinet had adopted the policy of free trade and favoured a new fiscal system which would be in close harmony with enlightened principles and with the needs of a new century. This policy would increase the friendship between nations. It seemed as if the principles of true political economy were being championed by the government of the world's leading commercial and maritime power. The economists had no hesitation in accepting these assurances and rejoiced in the imminent dawn of the golden age for which they had long been preparing the world. No minister of state was praised so much when he was alive and mourned so sincerely after his death than Canning. Yet it is very doubtful if this distinguished statesman had used his great intellectual gifts to further England's commercial supremacy – at everyone else's expense – rather than to promote the welfare of mankind.

The enlightened statesmen of the world had not such bright hopes for the future as to be prepared to accept the cosmopolitan catch-words of the English government as a basis for their own policy. They asked themselves what their countries would gain from handing over their industry to the tender mercies of the English in order to be graciously permitted to sell their surplus farm products in the English market. They asked themselves if the English government was really in a position to confer these benefits upon foreign countries. They asked themselves if the English landowners would agree to opening England's ports to foreign agricultural produce. They realised that such a policy might have to contend with very considerable opposition if its success depended entirely upon the support of a single minister, however able and popular he might be. They appreciated that this opposition might lead to the adoption of a very different fiscal policy. They realised that if the minister died he might be replaced by someone holding views of a very different kind. They saw that there might be a change in the policy of the occupant of the throne or his advisers. They reflected upon the unhappy consequences of such a change of policy for their own countries, which might have to leave industry in the lurch to give free trade a trial. In France in particular the disastrous consequences of the (Eden) Treaty of 1786 had not been forgotten. So these statesmen decided that it would be in their interests to postpone any decision for the time being and to refrain from co-operating (with England) until the policy of free trade had been more firmly established and had had an opportunity to develop.

An enlightened politician[1] once remarked that Huskisson's theory of free trade had not been intended for home consumption. It had been intended for export.

For the English free trade means that foreign farm products may be imported only when the country is threatened with famine. As far as manufactured goods are concerned Huskisson was steadfast in his support of the policy of protection while in his speeches he was always prepared to use the catchwords of the free traders. He did indeed reduce import duties on many manufactured goods but he never failed to ensure that the new import duties continued to give adequate protection to England's industries. He showed the same skill as the Dutch engineers who build high dykes where the water is high and low dykes where the water is low. They do not consider erecting dykes of uniform height. They simply build dykes which are high enough to protect the land from being flooded. Huskisson also repealed some useless ancient laws and this – with a few tariff changes – was all that came of the attempt to put the English theory of free trade into practice.

---

1. [List was referring to Henry Baldwin (1780-1844), Associate Justice of the United States Supreme Court between 1830 and 1844. In a speech to Congress on April 21, 1820 Baldwin had declared that the books of English economists "are for exportation not for home consumption". In *The National System of Political Economy*, 1841, List wrote: "a highly accomplished American orator, Mr. Baldwin, Chief Justice of the United States, when referring to the Canning-Huskisson system of free trade, shrewdly remarked, that, like most English productions, it had been manufactured not so much for home consumption as for exportation" (translation of 1885: new edition, 1966, p. 74 note 1).]

CHAPTER TWENTY EIGHT

History of France's Economic Policy

ENGLAND'S great success aroused the ambitions of France. At a time when Germany and Holland had many flourishing manufacturing and commercial cities, the French had not made very much progress with regard to trade and industry.

Early in the sixteenth century Francis I introduced from Milan the cultivation of mulberry trees and the manufacture of silk.[1] Since silk was a luxury product, which was very expensive at that time, only small quantities were consumed and the output of silk could not be compared with the output of woollen or linen cloth. Henry IV encouraged the manufacture of linen and woollen cloth and glassware by persuading Flemish artisans to settle in France. He also endeavoured to encourage the silk industry. After he had suppressed the nobles Cardinal Richelieu turned his attention to the economy and he tried to stimulate the expansion of trade and industry. He fostered the growth of the manufacture of silks, velvets, and woollens in Rouen. He founded trading companies, encouraged the fishing industry, and created a splendid fleet. Subsequently Cardinal Mazarin promoted the establishment of cloth workshops in Sedan by granting important privileges to the manufacturers – including even patents of nobility. But all Mazarin's efforts had insignificant results compared with the achievements of Colbert in Louis XIV's reign.

When this great statesman took office the French fleet had been ruined. The state no longer protected industry. There was a depression in agriculture. Commerce was restricted by provincial customs duties. The public finances were in a state of disorder.

1. [The silk industry was introduced into France at an earlier date than that given by List. Chaptal states in *De l'industrie françoise* (two volumes, 1819) that Louis XI had brought the silk industry to the Tours district (Vol I, p. 180). Louis XI reigned from 1461 to 1483]

Colbert was the son of a cloth merchant and had practical experience of trade and industry. He combined great talents with an energetic character. He embarked upon a policy of radical economic reforms. He subsidised the main branches of manufacture; he persuaded skilled foreign workers to settle in France; he purchased models of new machines as well as the secrets of foreign industrialists; he tried to replace provincial customs duties by a national tariff;[1] and he placed heavy import duties upon manufactured goods that could be made at home. By these means this great statesman promoted the growth of industry in France to such an extent that ten years after he had taken office the woollen industry had over 50,000 handlooms while the trade in silk was valued at 50,000,000 francs a year. Colbert created a navy of 198 ships manned by 166,000 men. He increased the national revenue by 28,000,000 francs.

Despite these great successes the doctrinaire French economists have criticised Colbert for having favoured industry at the expense of agriculture, which they allege was oppressed by his policy. Some of them have actually gone so far as to declare that Colbert's policy has cost France some important branches of industry, which moved to England and to the Low Countries. If ever a man has been accused of a crime when, in fact, he showed the qualities of the highest statesmanship, that man was Colbert. But the arguments of his critics are either senseless or are founded upon erroneous premises.[2]

1. [Colbert did not introduce a national tariff covering the whole of France. On the eve of the revolution in 1789 there were three tariff regions in France: (i) the 5 Great Farms (Colbert's tariff union of 1664), (ii) the provinces "reputed to be foreign", and (iii) the provinces "actually foreign". See Map 40 in Vries, Luykx, and Henderson, *An Atlas of World History* (1965).]
2. [List's note] We cite here Adam Smith's judgement of Colbert. In view of what we have said above we do not consider that we need to comment upon Adam Smith's criticism. Adam Smith wrote in *The Nature and Causes of the Wealth of Nations*: "Mr Colbert, the famous minister of Louis XIV, was a man of probity, of great industry, and knowledge of detail; of great experience and acuteness in the examination of public accounts, and of abilities in short, every way fitted for introducing method and good order into the collection and expenditure of the public revenue. That minister had unfortunately embraced all the prejudices of the mercantile system, in its nature and essence a system of restraint and regulation, and such as could scarce fail to be agreeable to a laborious and plodding man of business, who had been accustomed to regulate the different departments of public offices, and to establish the necessary checks and controls for confining each to its proper sphere. The industry and commerce of a great country he endeavoured to regulate upon the same model as the

To do full justice to Colbert it should be remembered that agriculture in France was hampered by a thousand restrictions during the period of his great reforms. Peasants had to perform forced labour (*corvée*) for their lords and they had to pay tithes to the Church. They were forbidden to change the rotation of their crops or to introduce new crops. They had to pay heavy dues to their lords and – indirectly through their landlords – they paid taxes to the nobility. The nobles hunted over the land cultivated by the peasants. The peasants were even forbidden to kill game which threatened to destroy their crops. Yet when the lord of the manor went hunting, the peasants were liable to perform forced labour for him. Condorcet – I think in his life of Turgot – tells a story of a peasant, accused of killing a wild boar, who made the excuse that he thought he was defending himself against a man.[1] The peasants lacked education and were deprived of their freedom. They were universally regarded with contempt. The ignorance and arrogance of the nobles and the public officials, the fanaticism of the clergy, the sharp divisions between different regions brought about by provincial dues, and – above all – the wretched state of communications were the real reasons for the decay of agriculture. Colbert's national tariff and the growth of the woollen and silk industries had nothing to do with the decline of farming in France at this time. Any sensible person can appreciate that the large number of silk workshops, fostered by Colbert and protected by tariffs, helped to stimulate both agriculture and other branches of industry. It is a fact, now universally recognised, that nothing encourages the expansion of agriculture so much as the establishment of manufacturing enterprises. Even Adam Smith and Say admit that farmers can flourish only if they have a market for their produce in an industrial town. Although Colbert restricted the export of agricultural products he provided them with a large internal market. We do not defend restrictions on the export of agricultural products, which are no

---

departments of a public office; and instead of allowing every man to pursue his own interest in his own way, upon the liberal plan of equality, liberty, and justice, he bestowed upon certain branches of industry extraordinary privileges, while he laid others under as extraordinary restraints. He was not only disposed, like other European ministers, to encourage more the industry of the towns than that of the country; but, in order to support the industry of the towns, he was willing even to depress and keep down that of the country". (Everyman Edition, Vol. II, p. 157).

1. [The story does not appear in Condorcet's life of Turgot.]

doubt highly undesirable.[1] Despite this mistake it is clear that Colbert greatly stimulated French agriculture. We have already explained why French agriculture did not flourish as much as Colbert's opponents desired. After Colbert left office industry no longer prospered as it had done during his administration. Was it his fault that no new Colbert appeared on the scene to carry on his work? Was it his fault that France did not have a constitution, similar to that of England, which would have enabled a sound permanent fiscal system to be established? In France, however, everything depended upon the king's pleasure. Was it Colbert's fault that the spirit of reform perished with the death of the reformer? After Colbert's death all the capacities of the country were monopolised by the royal court. While manufacturers and craftsmen were despised, the most idle and useless members of society were held in high esteem. The fanaticism and extravagance of Louis XIV were enough to destroy the work of ten Colberts.[2]

The religious persecutions began in Colbert's lifetime. They put an end to any hope of attracting foreign capital and skilled artisans to France. They put an end to any confidence in the permanence of Colbert's reforms. Colbert died in 1683 and two years later Louis XIV revoked the Edict of Nantes. This cruel measure affected manufacturers and artisans more than anyone else because the most enlightened entrepreneurs and skilled workers were Huguenots. Some 500,000 refugees are estimated to have fled the country in the

1. [List's note] Chaptal shows clearly in the introduction to *De l'industrie Françoise* (two volumes, 1819) that Colbert's policy was a wise one. Colbert used the best means at his disposal in the circumstances of his day. It is Colbert's successors who should be criticised for failing to move with the times. When one considers that for a long time France was governed by despotic rulers who were opposed to any change one must regard Colbert as a wiser man than his critics. At a particular stage in social development despotic measures promote human progress in general and the development of industry in particular. Was not even slavery necessary to accustom men to work?

2. [List's note]. Mignet, with characteristic perspicacity and concision, writes as follows on Louis XIV's administration (*Histoire de la révolution française*, Vol. I, ch. 1): "The immense power which Louis XIV exercised at home against the heretics overflowed abroad against all Europe. Oppression was advised by ambitious counsellors and was carried out by dragoons whose success encouraged still more opporession. The complaints of the French people were smothered by victory laurels, and their groans were drowned by the cries of the victors. But eventually the men of genius died, the money disappeared, and it was clearly seen that tyranny had exhausted its resources by its own successes and had devoured its own future in advance". [This passage appears in Mignet's introduction and not in his first chapter.]

first three years after the revocation of the Edict of Nantes. It may well be that no Protestant state in the world has failed to gain the greatest possible benefits from this flight of the Huguenots from France. Elsewhere – on the banks of the Rhine, in Switzerland, Saxony, Prussia, the Low Countries, Denmark, Sweden, Russia, and America – the descendants of these refugees are today running the most important industries, which they inherited from their forefathers who were driven out of France. In Germany there are many towns where the manufacture of woollens, silks, and jewellery dates from the arrival of these skilled artisans from beyond the Rhine who had been forced to leave their native land. Even in the Cape of Good Hope their descendants now cultivate the vines which their forefathers introduced into that colony.

It is most unfair to Colbert to blame him for the faults of the French constitution, the stupidity of the government, the lack of patriotism of the aristocrats, and the fury of the religious fanatics.

Both France and England adopted a policy of protection but they did so under very different circumstances and with very different results. England was a century ahead of France and enjoyed many advantages such as an active and intelligent population, an enlightened aristocracy, a free constitution, a long period of uninterrupted peace, an island location, many rich overseas possessions, a large fleet, and a revolution which had swept away numerous abuses. The stability of England's fiscal system was guaranteed by the existence of a representative parliament. France, on the other hand, suffered from all the drawbacks of a despotic administration; costly wars; a licentious and bigoted clergy; an arrogant, extravagant, and uncouth aristocracy; and a slavish and ignorant population. So we see that the same fiscal system made England prosperous but left France backward. Political bodies may be compared with human bodies. If either is given a stimulant before the cause of a sickness has been removed, the stimulant will make the patient worse and not better. France had an excellent fiscal system which seemed likely to have beneficial results. It could have raised France to a position among the leading industrial countries of the world. But Louis XIV was no Henry IV. He drove half a million skilled artisans out of France instead of persuading half a million skilled workers to settle in France. He failed to free agriculture from its chains. He did not give the country sound institutions or good roads and canals. And so the policy of protection was attacked by

145

the theory of free trade – a doctrine continually gaining more adherents though it was forced to rely upon the most ridiculous arguments. The world was not ready for this doctrine and will not be for a very long time. Although Adam Smith's version of the free trade theory turned it into a foreign dogma it might have had a chance of being put into practice in France. Yet in England not a single statesman was converted to Adam Smith's views.

We would like to refer at this point to the relations between the disciples of Quesnay and those of Adam Smith. Although Adam Smith destroyed the foundations of the doctrines of the Physiocrats, he accepted the principle of free trade which they advocated. Adam Smith gave the doctrine the support of his great authority. He was therefore cautious in his criticisms of the Physiocrats. He praised the nobility of their sentiments and he approved the grandeur of their aims. He persuaded them to accept his doctrines. He resembles the captain of a warship who captures an enemy vessel and then praises the gallantry of his foes so as to persuade them to enter his service.

It was a misfortune for France that some of Quesnay's disciples came to hold high public office. The most famous was Turgot, whose great talents and abilities led to his appointment as Minister of the Interior. Although he held high principles and enlightened views he fell under the spell of the reforming philosophers who – in their determination to better the human race and to improve political institutions – failed to differentiate between what was new and what was true. They promulgated abstract principles without taking sufficient account of what was happening in the real world and so they made the mistake of adopting extreme policies. France had cause to be grateful for Turgot's administration since he proposed to break the chains that fettered her industry, and – above all – her agriculture. On the other hand France suffered severely as a result of his administration since he advocated an industrial policy which was the exact opposite of that pursued by Colbert. Turgot accepted the validity of the two main principles advocated by the doctrinaire economists. The first was that taxes should be levied only on the land – or rather upon the income derived from the land – since, in the view of the Physiocrats, agriculture alone produces wealth. The second was that the best way to stimulate agriculture was to reduce import duties on foreign products as much as possible. In this way Turgot came to champion unrestricted free trade between all countries. It was largely through the influence of Turgot's writings that, by the end of Louis XVI's reign, it was widely held by enlightened Frenchmen that only a commercial treaty with England could save the country from the consequences of a huge national debt and an enormous budget deficit.

England is ever ready to profit from the misfortunes of others – whether the misfortunes are due to a lack of physical resources or (as in this case) to a lack of political judgment. England was very happy to bestow upon France the blessings of a new edition of the Methuen Treaty. So in 1786 the Eden Treaty was signed[1] which reduced the English import duties on French wine and brandy and opened the French market to English manufactured goods. The French waited impatiently for the favourable results of this agreement that they had been promised by the enlightened philosophers. But they soon experienced the very opposite from what they had been led to believe would happen. The great experiment ended with the experience of the dog in the fable who lost his bone because he grasped at a shadow. The English, having been used to drinking Portuguese wines for over a hundred years, did not greatly increase their consumption of French wines. On the other hand the French market was flooded with cheap English manufactured goods. The English controlled vast resources of capital and could grant favourable credit terms to their customers. Consequently they were strong enough to drive French manufacturers out of their own home market. Moreover the French could offer the English only luxury products and the total value of these goods was relatively small. But the English could sell in France goods in every-day use, which had a much greater total value. The treaty had been in force for only a few years when the French government appreciated that French industry had been brought to the brink of ruin and terminated the agreement. The ending of the Eden Treaty had some very disagreeable consequences for the French but not for the English. It was obviously difficult to revive the ruined industries of France but it was a simple matter to persuade a few palates, which had become accustomed to French wines to start drinking Portuguese wines again. But the French had become accustomed to English manufactured goods and now secured them through the activities of smugglers. Many French manufacturers were ruined at the very

1. [For the Eden Treaty see W. O. Henderson, *The Genesis of the Common Market* (Frank Cass, 1962), ch. 2.]

time when they most needed help from the government. Sir Walter Scott did not include this wretched treaty in his list of the causes of the French revolution[1] but Princess Lamballe did appreciate the significance of the Eden Treaty – a striking example of how an observant lady at court can do better than the most famous novelist of our time.[2]

When the Jacobins overthrew the ancien régime they destroyed the good with the bad because they had neither the time nor the ability to appreciate where the true commercial interests of France lay. These idiots dreamed of establishing a new Roman Republic and since the Romans had despised industry and valued only agriculture, the Jacobins considered only those who worked on the land to be true republicans. But Napoleon thought otherwise. No one can doubt his genius, though one may criticise his propensity for despotism, and his boundless egotism. As soon as he came to power, he realised that, under existing circumstances, no country can hope to attain a high level of power, prosperity, and independence, unless it possesses flourishing industries. He appreciated that – when faced with the rivalry of more advanced industrial countries – industrial progress could be achieved only by the imposition of import duties and by other encouragements by the state.

In his usual trenchant style Napoleon made the following comment upon the policy of free trade: "If an empire was built upon granite, it would crumble into dust if it introduced free trade".

Napoleon not only revived the old prohibitions and restrictions on foreign imports to stimulate French industry but he extended them all over the Continent in the hope of weakening and defeating the most powerful of his enemies. The success of both aspects of Napoleon's policy is proved first by the vigour of England's counter measures, and secondly by the way in which industry prospered in all countries covered by the Continental System – despite the exceptionally heavy burdens which these countries had to shoulder during the war.

In the previous chapter we discussed Lord Castlereagh's failure to take advantage of England's victory over the Continental System, and we explained how Canning and Huskisson, as soon as they came to power, decided to repair Castlereagh's omission. They

1. [Sir Walter Scott, *Life of Napoleon Buonaparte, Emperor of the French, with a Preliminary View of the French Revolution* (9 vols., 1827).]
2. [Mme Guénard (ed.), *Mémoires de la Princesse de Lamballe* (4 vols., 1801).]

proclaimed the adoption of a new fiscal policy and pretended to support the doctrine of free trade. No doubt they hoped that other countries would reduce their import duties and so enable England to flood their markets with still more manufactured goods.

Just as in 1786, when England had been supported by the enlightened philosophers and their disciples, so on this occasion was England aided by the cosmopolitan economists, who were delighted with the doctrine of free trade. Dazzled by the brilliance of the writings of J. B. Say – a man as honourable in his beliefs and policies as Turgot – the economists denounced as fools and knaves all who rejected the infallibility of the free trade doctrine or who refused to believe in the truly philanthropic policy of Canning and Huskisson. The same thing had happened 50 years ago when every economist or politician who wished to be really up to date, was compelled to believe in free trade as a universal panacea which would cure all the ills that afflicted mankind.

Whatever criticism may be made of the Restoration government in France there can be no doubt that it deserves the thanks of industry. The Restoration government was not deflected from its support of the policy of protection by the intrigues of the English government, the howls of the opposition, or the egotistical demands of the merchants and the owners of vineyards.

When Canning visited Paris to propose to the French government a renewal of the commercial treaty of 1786 M. de Villèle made it clear that he was well aware of the consequences of trade agreements of the Methuen type. It is said that he told Canning that the level of English import duties was just right to protect English industry from foreign competition. Since French industries had not yet made sufficient progress to compete successfully with foreign rivals they still needed the protection of a tariff just as a sapling must be safeguarded against the first blast of wind that threatens to blow it down. Once a point had been reached when French industries no longer feared foreign competition Villèle would not fail to take advantage of Canning's proposals.

Canning's conduct when he returned to England showed that Villèle must have said something of the sort. He ceased to proclaim the coming of free trade. When the problem of Spain was discussed in Parliament he threw courtesy and diplomacy to the wind and boasted that by giving France the task of sending troops to Spain he had hung a millstone round her neck. This remark shows how

Canning proposed to avenge himself upon Villèle. It shows also that his policy was neither so enlightened nor so philanthropic as the trusting liberals on the Continent wanted the world to believe. In fact Canning was every inch an Englishman whose philanthropy lasted just so long as it accorded with England's commercial supremacy.[1]

It needed no great perspicacity on the part of M. de Villèle to avoid the trap that had been laid for him. On the one hand he could see that Germany's industry, agriculture, and flocks of sheep, which had prospered greatly under the protection of the Continental System, had now seriously declined partly because of England's policy of prohibitions and partly because of English competition in Germany's own home market. On the other hand he could see that experts who were independent of any political affiliations and were recognised authorities on the state of French industry – men like Chaptal and Baron Dupin – had provided ample evidence to warrant the continued protection of French industry.

Chaptal's book on French industry champions the policy of protection from cover to cover and gives numerous details of the success achieved by this policy. It seems as if the whole book was written as an expansion of the following passage:

> Instead of losing ourselves in a labyrinth of metaphysical abstractions we recommend the maintenance and the extension of the

1. [List's note] In his *Cours complet d'économie politique*, Part III, p. 363 Say wrote: "In England the House of Commons appeared to recognise the validity of the warnings given by knowledgeable men that great harm would be done to industry and commerce by the excessive use of the fiscal system of prohibitions. This policy was partially – though not entirely – abandoned and its effects were considerably mitigated. It is curious that although the prohibitive system was regarded as successful in certain respects, nevertheless the English are trying to get rid of it on the ground that it hampers the progress of their industries".

Augustus Granville Stapleton in his biography of Canning (Part IV, p. 3) writes as follows about the views of this great statesman on free trade: "Mr. Canning was perfectly convinced of the truth of the abstract principle, that commerce is sure to flourish most, when wholly unfettered by restrictions, but since such had not been the opinions, either of our ancestors or of surrounding nations and since in consequence restraints had been imposed upon all commercial transactions, a state of things had grown up, to which the unguarded application of the abstract principle, however true it was in theory might have been somewhat mischievous in practice. The opposite course, however, if entirely disregarding this principle in commercial legislation, would certainly have been less mischievous in its ultimate results and Mr. Canning felt that it was the part of a sound policy never indeed to lose sight of the principle, but at the same time never to forget that from the circumstance of its having been previously lost sight of, there existed an absolute necessity for applying it with discretion and care". Canning spoke one way and acted another.

existing fiscal policy. A sound tariff is a sure safeguard for industry and agriculture. The import duties levied at our frontiers should be increased or lowered according to circumstances. The tariff compensates our manufacturers for the high wages that they pay and for the high cost of fuel. Prohibitions protect industries from foreign competition during their infancy. The policy of protection defends the independence of our industries and enriches France by safeguarding the labour of its people which, as I have often observed, is the national wealth.

The excellent book of Charles Dupin on France's productive powers was a pioneer work. Dupin was the first to examine the economy and the constitution of France from the point of view of the nation's productive powers. In another book on the growth of France's productive powers since 1814 he showed clearly how much France has benefitted from the Continental System and from the fiscal policy of protection pursued by the government of the Restoration. It is obvious that no French government, whoever its leaders may be, would dare to ruin the success of the last 40 years – achieved at such great sacrifices and so hopeful for the future – by signing a new Methuen Treaty with England.

Dupin gives the following examples to illustrate France's economic progress between 1812 and 1827: The population rose by 4 million in that period. The number of sheep increased by 5 million and the number of horses by 400,000. The output of woollens rose from 70 to 100 million lbs, cotton from 20 to 64 million lbs, pig iron from 200 to 320 million lbs. France imported sheep from Leicester and Nubia (the Sudan) and goats from Tibet and produced the wool from which large numbers of Kashmir shawls were made. Silk worms were brought from China which produced a fine white silk and considerable quantities of silks were exported to Turkey and Persia, which once sent their silks to France. The population of Lyons, the chief centre for the manufacture of silk rose from 100,000 to 150,000. Paris alone exported (annually) manufactured goods to the value of 47 million (francs). France has overtaken England in the production of printed cottons and in all kind of machines. France has overtaken Germany in printed cottons, fine damask, Prussian blue dye, steelware, and printing. France has overtaken Turkey in red dye, India in silks, Persia in shawls, Switzerland in clocks, watches and mathematical instruments. France has greatly improved the quality of her steel, copper,

151

tin and platinum and has achieved considerable success in the printing of books, the printing of cloth (cottons, woollens and silks) and the manufacture of pottery and chinaware. France leads the world in the production of porcelain, carpets, and chemical products. In view of this great growth in her productive powers France has nearly doubled her internal commerce and has considerably expanded her foreign trade.

The author regrets that time does not permit him to add here a long note on the silk trade between France and England.[1]

CHAPTER TWENTY NINE

History of Germany's Economic Policy[2]

THE FREE CITIES of Italy had inherited the civilisation of the ancient world and had been neighbours of the Byzantine Empire which, even in decline, still had – in comparison with the barbarians of northern Europe – preserved some of the intellectual and artistic achievements of the Roman Empire. During the crusades, at a time when the Italian cities had already made considerable progress in all branches of industry, religious zeal further stimulated the productive powers which they had already developed. Their ships were constantly employed to transport the armies of the crusaders to Palestine. The crusaders brought back with them new inventions,

1. [This sentence was added by Emilie List after the manuscript had been completed.]
2. [List's note] Fischer, *Histoire du commerce de l'Allemagne*; Sartorius, *Histoire de la Ligue Hans*; Lambeccius, *Origines Hamb*; Angl. a Werdenhagen [sic], *de rebus publ. hans tractus*. [Full references: F.C.J. Fischer, *Geschichte des teutschen Handels*... (4 vols, Hanover, 1785-91); Georg Sartorius, *Geschichte des Hanseatischen Bundes* (3 vols., Göttingen, 1802-8); P. Lembeccius, *Origines Hamburgenses, sive Rebus Hamburgensium* (Vol. 2, Hamburg, 1706); J.A. Werdenhagen, *De rebus publicis Hanseaticis* ... (1631). List may have derived his knowledge of the books of Lambeccius and Werdenhagen from quotations in Adam Anderson, *An Historical and Chronological Deduction of the Origin of Commerce* (6 vols, Dublin, 1790).]

plants, methods of cultivation, and crafts. They cultivated new tastes and found new sources of enjoyment. The goods which were most sought after in the West had always been those produced in the East. They reached Europe by way of the Red Sea, the Nile, Alexandria, and Venice. The merchants of Venice distributed these goods throughout northern Europe. They were sent by land to the valley of the Rhine and by sea to the ports of France, England, Flanders, and Germany. Alternative routes by which these goods reached northern Europe began in Persia and went to Aleppo or Constantinople either overland or by sea through the Persian Gulf (Basra).

It has been the experience of all ages and of all countries that freedom and industrial progress are like siamese twins. Wherever industry starts to develop there is a movement in favour of political freedom. And whenever the flag of liberty is hoisted there will be no delay in the appearance of industry. It is axiomatic that the acquisition of wealth brings with it a demand for security to enjoy it. Similarly as soon as people attain a measure of freedom they use their freedom and their skills to improve their living standards. Since wealth enables people to obtain – or to purchase – freedom, we find that in medieval times the progress of industry and the progress of liberty followed closely in the footsteps of the expansion of commerce along the valley of the Rhine to the Low Countries, to the coasts of the Baltic, and to the very heart of the barbarous regions in the East where Novgorod became a city with republican institutions. The future prosperity of Flanders was assured when its Count cleared the district of brigands at an early date and established the cloth industry with the help of Italian artisans. In Germany the founding of cities began in the tenth century, when the Emperor Henry I, desirous of strengthening his dominions, fostered urban expansion throughout his territories. The same policy was followed, from political motives, by his successors for many hundreds of years. Like some judicious French and English monarchs, these Emperors regarded the cities as powerful allies against the nobles, as a rich source of income, and as the basis for national defence. The social life of the towns fostered the growth of arts and crafts. Wealthy burghers promoted municipal liberty, a spirit of enterprise, and the pursuit of knowledge. Of their own free will the Emperors granted charters to the towns which gave the citizens the rights enjoyed by those living under republican rule.

As far as the towns were concerned the powers exercised by the Emperors were restricted to matters of national importance. As early as the tenth and eleventh centuries there was an astonishing activity on the coasts of Germany and the Low Countries. New cities were founded which rapidly expanded; new commercial links were forged between towns; while municipal institutions became more efficient. The progress of German towns at this time cannot be better described than by comparing their growth with urban developments in North America in recent years. In the early middle ages Germany – particularly the northern cities – expanded with youthful vigour and zest.

The municipalities, continually threatened by the brigandage of the nobles on land and by the pirates on the high seas, decided to unite to defend their common interests. Hamburg and Lübeck formed an alliance in 1241 and before the end of the thirteenth century this union had grown so that it included 85 towns in the interior of Germany and on the coasts of the North Sea and the Baltic. This federation was called the Hanseatic League. In the old German dialect "Hansa" meant "federation" or "alliance". The members of this league soon benefitted by using their united strength to foster the expansion of their commerce. They developed a commercial policy, the success of which was soon evident in the unparalleled prosperity of their trade and shipping.

Realising the need to protect their shipping the Hansa Towns established a powerful navy. They appreciated that the strength or weakness of a country's sea power depends upon the strength or weakness of its fisheries and merchant shipping. Consequently the Hansa Towns fostered their fishing industry and forbade members to transport their goods in any ships save those belonging to the towns themselves.

Although the commerce of the Hansa Towns was in the hands of private companies, the League debated and promulgated laws and regulations as if it was a sovereign independent state. It concluded commercial treaties with foreign countries and authorised the establishment of factories and warehouses abroad. Charters were issued concerning the orderly conduct of business in these establishments. The League received envoys from foreign countries and sent ambassadors abroad. It organised and maintained the means for common defence. It introduced a system of uniform weights and measures. Although controlled by merchants the League found it necessary to impose various restrictions upon the way in which commerce should be conducted.

When the Hansa merchants came to London they found that it was a miserable place with wooden thatched hovels. People lived in rooms that were worse than stables. At that time England was the America of the Hanseatic League. The Hansa merchants sent manufactured goods to England in exchange for wool, skins, butter, lead, and tin.

The Hanseatic League set up a second factory at Bruges in Flanders in 1252. This was the great market for the sale of the raw materials that the Hansa merchants brought from England and Russia in exchange for their manufactured products and goods from the East. In Flanders the English wool was turned into cloth which was then sent back to England. A third factory was established in Novgorod in Russia, which sent furs, hemp, flax, tallow, and other raw materials to Germany. Finally a fourth factory was built in Bergen in Norway. This became the centre of the Hanseatic fishing industry. The sailors employed by the Hanseatic merchants were trained in the fishing grounds.

All countries, once they have emerged from a state of barbarism, have experienced the situation in which they derive great benefits from trading freely with a more advanced industrialised country. But later this relationship becomes a burden which hampers the development of its own manufacturers. England experienced this and Edward IV introduced a commercial policy of prohibitions which culminated in the expulsion of the Hansa merchants from English soil by Queen Elizabeth.

At the beginning of Elizabeth's reign the Hansa merchants were not satisfied with maintaining their existing privileges but complained bitterly of their treatment at the hands of Edward VI and Queen Mary. Elizabeth prudently replied that it was not in her power to change the existing state of affairs but that she would be prepared to allow the Hansa merchants to continue to enjoy the rights that they still possessed. The Hansa merchants were far from satisfied. In the hope of avenging themselves and of punishing Elizabeth, they broke off all trade with England. This action, however, benefitted the English merchants who took advantage of the situation, to expand their trading operations. The Hansa merchants, beside themselves with rage, did everything in their power to discredit the English traders with other countries. They secured the promulgation of an Imperial Edict which prohibited English merchants from trading anywhere in the Holy Roman Empire. Queen Elizabeth sought to avenge herself by seizing 60 Hanseatic vessels, laden with Spanish contraband in the River Thames. She proposed to free these vessels as part of a bargain with the Hanseatic League. When it became known that a conference of Hansa towns had been held at Lübeck to discuss measures to destroy England's overseas trade, Elizabeth confiscated the ships and their cargoes. Only two ships were released so that a message from the Queen, condemning the policy of the League, could reach the Hansa towns.

That was the way in which Elizabeth treated the merchants who had lent her father – and many earlier kings – ships with which to fight England's naval battles. These were the merchants who had for centuries been courted by all the rulers in Europe. These were the merchants who had acted as arbiters in the struggles between Sweden and Denmark. These were the merchants who had put a king on the Swedish throne and had made him their vassal. These were the merchants who had chased a King of Denmark off his throne and had auctioned it to the highest bidder. These were the merchants who, by force of arms, had forced monarchs to recognise their privileges and who, more than once, had held the crown of England in pawn as a pledge for the repayment of loans granted to the king. These were the merchants who had destroyed Copenhagen and had actually carried their arrogance and ferocity so far as to let hundreds of English fishermen drown when they dared to invade the Hanseatic fishing grounds off Bergen.

Although the Hansa merchants were still strong enough to avenge Elizabeth's insults they were by this time beginning to lose their former powers. When they begged for new privileges from all the courts of Europe, their pleas were contemptuously rejected. In 1630 the Hanseatic League, which had once been capable of striking terror in men's hearts, was formally dissolved.

There were many reasons for the decline and fall of the Hanseatic League. Denmark and Sweden damaged the interests of the Hansa towns whenever they could in revenge for the former presumptuous policy of the German merchants. The Czar turned them out of Russia and granted trading privileges to an English company. The Teutonic Order, for many years an ally of the Hanseatic League, was vanquished and destroyed by the Poles. In the days of their power and prosperity the Hansa towns had ignored the Holy Roman Empire. Now, when it was too late, they remembered the existence of the Imperial Diet and laid their grievances before it. Werdenhagen states that the Hanseatic merchants complained to the Imperial Diet that England was exporting 200,000 pieces of cloth annually, most of which was sold in Germany. The only way to force Elizabeth to come to terms with the Hanseatic League would be to ban English cloths from Germany. The Imperial Diet agreed to do this but – according to Anderson – Mr (George) Gilpin, the English ambassador to the Diet, devised a stratagem to prevent the edict from being carried out.[1]

The wisdom of the principle "Laissez faire et laissez passer" was not exactly confirmed by the history of the Hansa towns because after the towns had allowed the merchants to go their own way, the merchants in turn left the towns in the lurch as soon as it became clear that there was no profit to be made by staying. At a time when the Dutch were said to be building 2,000 ships a year there were Hamburg merchants who sold their ships in Venice and settled in Holland on the proceeds.

The glory and importance of so magnificent a commercial empire as that of the Hanseatic League justifies us in examining the causes of its decline and fall more closely.

The commerce of these towns had no national basis. It was not based upon any balance of the various branches of native industry and it was not supported by an adequate political power. The bonds which linked the members of the League were too weak for the interests of the burghers of particular towns to be subordinated to the interests of the League as a whole. This fatal divergence of local municipal interests led to jealousies and even to betrayals. Cologne, for example, repeatedly used the enmity between England and the League to her own advantage. Hamburg adopted a similar policy with regard to a dispute between Lübeck and Denmark. If taxes were due, no one had any funds available. If booty was to be distributed every town tried to get as much as possible for itself. The commerce of the League was not based upon home production and consumption – German agriculture and industry – but was no more

1. [Anderson, citing Werdenhagen, wrote: "Yet Gilpin by a stratagem, outwitted the Hanseatics in such sort, that the sentence could not be executed till the decision of another Diet; and our merchants were afterwards permitted to remove from Stade to Hamburg, where they were well received" (*An Historical and Chronological Deduction of the Origin of Commerce*, op. cit., Vol. II, p. 206 *et. seq.*).]

than an enormous transit trade. The League protected and fostered a variety of economic activities such as farming in Poland, sheep rearing in England, iron-ore mining in Sweden, copper mining in Russia and various industries in the Low Countries. For centuries the Hansa merchants put into practice the theory of our modern doctrinaire economists. They bought in the cheapest market and sold in the dearest. But when the Hansa merchants were turned out of the countries in which they bought and sold, they could not fall back upon a new field for the investment of their capital in Germany because German agriculture and industry – which they had neglected in their days of great prosperity – had not developed sufficiently. And so the wealth of the Hansa merchants was attracted to Holland and to England where it actually fostered the power, the wealth, and the industrial development of their enemies.

The Hanseatic League failed to secure for itself a permanent influence over the constitutional development under the protection of the Imperial Diet. All went well so long as the League had money and sea power. The Emperor, the kings and the princes were good friends of the League but they also feared its power. In vain did Emperor Sigismund try to protect his relative King Eric of Denmark. The League simply ignored him and the Emperor dared not openly express his anger at this total lack of respect for the Imperial dignity. In practice the Hanseatic League acted like a sovereign state. But when the League lost its sea power, it also lost its influence over the Imperial Diet. Moreover the nobles, long jealous of the power of the League, boldly demanded that "the Emperor should suppress the great trading companies, which rule the country through their wealth". One by one the Hansa towns in the interior of Germany fell under the influence of the nobles and so the Hansa ports lost the basis of their power in the heart of the country.

The English avoided all these mistakes. In England political power, national independence, and private industry progressed hand in hand. Agriculture and industry provided a firm foundation for trade and shipping. Internal commerce was six times greater than foreign trade which is as it should be. Yet England's foreign trade was more important than that of any other country. The interests of the crown, the nobility and the towns coincided in the most fortunate manner. Would any sensible person, who reflects upon the progress of England's industries deny that without the application of national power to the expansion of the economy, England would never have attained so remarkable a standard of efficiency – and so high a degree of self-sufficiency – in shipping and industry? Of course not. But for the prudent policy of England's rulers, the Hansa merchants might still be in the Steelyard in London. They might still be buying wool and selling cloth. England, with her great flocks of sheep, might still be the sheep-run of the Hansa towns, just as Portugal, by the cunning of English diplomacy, has become England's vineyard. Indeed it is possible that, without government aid to industrial progress, the English might never have secured the political freedom that they enjoy today. English liberties are the fruits of England's industry and wealth.

When one examines the rivalry and the struggle between the Hanseatic League and England it is surprising to discover that Adam Smith never discusses the development of the League from its foundation to its fall, although it is clear from several of his observations, that he is very well acquainted with the history of the Hansa Towns. Adam Smith writes:

> A merchant it has been said very properly, is not necessarily the citizen of any particular country. It is in a great measure indifferent to him from what place he carries on his trade; and a very trifling disgust will make him remove his capital, and together with it all the industry which it supports, from one country to another. No part of it can be said to belong to any particular country, till it has been spread as it were over the face of that country, either in buildings or in the lasting improvement of lands. No vestige now remains of the great wealth said to have been possessed by the greater part of the Hansa towns except in the obscure histories of the thirteenth and fourteenth centuries. It is even uncertain where some of them were situated or to what towns in Europe the Latin names given to some of them belong.

It is indeed astonishing that Adam Smith, who appreciated so clearly that the main reason for the fall of the Hansa towns was the emigration of their capitalists, should not have examined more thoroughly the causes of this movement of capital, which he ascribes to the commercial policy of England and Holland. It is surprising that he does not draw attention to the failure of the Hansa towns to adopt an enlightened commercial policy which might have created a national German commerce out of their own trade and industry. Such a policy would have enabled the Hansa towns to resist any attempt of foreign states to damage their trade by prohibitions and restrictions. It seems to me that the results of such an enquiry would hardly have provided much support for Adam Smith's main arguments.

After the disintegration of the Hanseatic League the trade and industry of Germany declined more and more. One of the main reasons for this was the decline in the power of the Emperor which went hand in hand with the deterioration of the towns. Small principalities were established as a result of these developments and they established customs frontiers which undermined and ruined all Germany's common institutions. Finally the principalities became sovereign states and so carved up the true sovereignty of the whole of Germany into little fragments. Both the authority of the Emperor and the independence of the towns disappeared. Now the German ports were no longer protected from foreign intervention. At the same time the opening of the Cape of Good Hope route to India, discovered by the Portuguese, robbed Venice of her monopoly of commerce in eastern commodities and consequently some German inland towns lost their former transit trade in eastern goods.

Luther's Reformation increased the already existing dangerous divisions in Germany to such an extent that all the political units in the Holy Roman Empire, most of the states, and the towns were divided into two hostile camps. This was the final blow that rendered impossible the co-operation (between different sections of the community) which German commerce needed. Germany's economic productive powers were ruined by the evil effects of a variety of factors – the monetary anarchy, the petty jealousies, the lack of strong political institutions, the lack of a fiscal policy of protection, the failure to establish good communications, and the absence of internal free trade. When Holland, once a part of the Holy Roman Empire, became independent, the estuary of Germany's greatest river fell into foreign hands and Germany was so weak at that time that it failed to appreciate the incalculable drawback of Holland becoming an independent state.

Napoleon's Continental System revived Germany's industrial activities, although it was a serious disadvantage that German manufactured goods were excluded from the French market and could no longer reach Spain, Portugal, or the Portuguese colonies.

Yet at the same time the German home market was wide open to French competition.

After the fall of Napoleon the English turned up again and monopolised the German market with their manufactured goods which were cheap and of high quality. Yet they simultaneously prohibited German raw materials from entering their home market or imposed high import duties on these products. So German industry was ruined again and there was even a marked decline in agriculture.

The customs union (*Zollverein*) of the German states was set up because Germany's commerce was placed in so disadvantageous a position in relation to France and England. This is a union of all the German states (except Austria, Brunswick, Hanover, Mecklenburg, Hamburg, Lübeck, and Bremen) and its aims are to secure complete freedom of internal trade and to establish a single tariff on foreign imports. The revenue from import duties is divided according to the respective populations of each state which is a member of the customs union. Since this customs union was established there has been a great expansion of Germany's industry, agriculture, and commerce.

The import duties of the Zollverein are generally calculated according to the weight of the goods concerned and so the duties which produce the largest revenues are those levied upon the commonest manufactured goods. Consequently the tariff protects particularly those industrial goods which are essential to the needs of the people. The total value of these goods is far greater than the value of imported luxury goods. The import duties are generally moderate. In addition to other products, Germany still imports 20 million (francs' worth) of cotton yarn and so her industries are still dependent upon other countries.

The commercial history of Germany shows that a people can be very industrious, very moral, very thrifty, very inventive, and very intelligent and can combine these qualities with the possession of a fruitful soil and many valuable natural resources, without however being able to attain a high standard of industrial, agricultural and commercial development. Indeed history teaches us that, in spite of all these advantages, there may actually be a decline in the economy simply because society is defective, weak, and divided. This weakness leads to a lack of security, laws, justice, freedom of movement and an absence of good communications, great markets, and trading companies. It leads also to a failure to open up markets abroad for her exports because the effects of foreign tariffs are ignored. Finally the failure to stimulate and to protect industry is the greatest weakness of all.

The history of the development of industry and commerce in Germany teaches us that the economic affairs of states which are not strong enough to erect and maintain a protective tariff fall under the control of the laws of other nations. Free trade is no more than an empty expression unless it is established and guaranteed by at least two countries. For centuries the German market has been open to the commerce of all nations. This passive freedom – this freedom to be injured by every disturber of the peace – has simply resulted in the ruin of the well-being of society.

History teaches us that there is nothing so important to a nation as the ability to take suitable measures to defend the country from invasion by foreign armies and by foreign goods. Failure to do this leads to the ruin of native industry once in every generation and to the need to start all over again by replacing what has been lost.

Finally history teaches us the complete inadequacy of the doctrines of the popular doctrinaire economists.

CHAPTER THIRTY

Economic Policy of Spain, Portugal and Italy[1]

WHILE THE ENGLISH built up their national industry on the most solid foundations, the Portuguese and the Spaniards grew rich through new discoveries overseas by which they became powerful

1. [List's note] Geronymo de Ustariz (*Théorie du commerce*) and Bernardo de Ulloa rightly attribute the depressed state of agriculture in Spain and the general collapse of economic prosperity to the ruin of industry. The causes which they mention for this decline include the provincial customs duties, local dues (*octrois*) and other ruinous taxes, the wretched state of the roads, the absence of canals, the importing of foreign goods, the prevalence of smuggling, and even the poor inns. But they remain silent on the two main reasons for Spain's decline – namely, despotism and fanaticism. Only Ustariz ventures to whisper a complaint about the vast sums sent annually to Rome. The flow of money to Rome would be of little consequence

nations in a short time. But the Portuguese and the Spaniards behaved like dissipated extravagant idlers who had won a big prize in a lottery, while the English were an industrious and thrifty people whose progress towards wealth and power, though slow, was solid and sure. Spendthrifts and gamblers who suddenly become very rich by chance will be able for a time to live in a more luxurious style than sober industrious workers. But when industrious people earn money by hard work their only ambition is to improve their position and to increase their knowledge still further. Those who acquire wealth rapidly are soon tempted to squander it in idle pleasures and so they destroy their own productive powers. A rich idler spoils his children who flatter his vanity and he fails to give them a good education. But a prudent man sees to it that his children are educated properly so as to give them the best possible opportunity to take over his business in due course and to expand it. Is it surprising that the descendants of the idlers are beggars while the descendants of the prudent man enjoy the rich fruits of their father's diligence and thrift?

The Spaniards possessed fine flocks of sheep so long ago that as early as 1172 Henry II of England forbade the importation of Spanish wool. Two centuries earlier the inhabitants of the Spanish district of Viscaya[1] were renowned for their production of iron and for their skill as sailors and fishermen. These people were undoubtedly the first to engage in whaling. As late as 1615 the English had to send fishermen to the Bay of Biscay to learn how to hunt whales. Spain was famed for her manufactured products from the earliest times until Colbert's day when she exported to France some of her fine woollen cloth. Spain had a great navy and mercantile marine and her large ships were for centuries feared by other sea powers. In short Spain possessed all the elements of future

---

but for the fact that Rome has deprived the Spaniards of the power to earn more money. [See Don Geronymo de Ustariz, *Theoria y pratica de commercio y de Marina* (1724, 1742, and 1757: English translation, 1757). List used the abridged French translation: *Traduction libre sur l'Espagnol de Don Geronymo de Ustariz...* (1753). See also Don Bernardo de Ulloa, *Restablicimiento de las fabricas y commercio espagnol* (1740). List used the French translation: Bernardo de Ulloa, *Rétablissement des manufactures et du commerce d'Espagne...* (Amsterdam, 1753). For Ustariz and Ulloa see Wirminghaus, *Zwei spanische Merkantilisten. G. de Ustariz and B. de Ulloa* (Jena, 1886).]

1. [Viscaya is the most northerly of the Basque provinces in Spain. It is on the Bay of Biscay and the chief town is Bilbao.]

economic prosperity when the growing national spirit was ruthlessly nipped in the bud by a combination of fanaticism and despotism. The first act of oppression by this unholy alliance was to expel the jews and the arabs – and even their descendants who had publicly given up their religious beliefs and had been converted to Catholicism. The expulsion of the jews and the arabs cost Spain many useful citizens and a great deal of capital. The fear inspired by the terrible practices of the Inquisition stopped foreigners from bringing their capital and manufacturing skills to Spain and actually compelled Spanish entrepreneurs to seek shelter in less dangerous countries. The discovery of the new world increased Spain's wealth but this was only an apparent and a purely temporary phenomenon which eventually actually hastened the utter ruin of the country. Spain failed to adopt the colonial policy later adopted by Holland and England. She failed to exchange the products of the new world for her own manufactured goods – a policy which is as much to the advantage of the colonies as to the mother country. Instead the Spaniards slaughtered and robbed the inhabitants of their colonies and then exchanged their ill-gotten gains for the manufactured products of foreign countries. Spain systematically turned people who had formerly been usefully occupied at home into brigands and oppressors in the new world. These evil deeds and oppressions led to a strengthening in the power and industry of other states, particularly the Low Countries. Spain actually fostered in her own territories her greatest foes and most prosperous rivals. In vain did the king promulgate laws and ordinances designed to foster Spanish industry and prevent bullion from leaving the country. The spirit of enterprise, economic progress, technical knowledge, and artistic skill develops only in countries enriched by political and religious freedom. Gold and silver remain only in countries where they can be usefully employed in active prosperous industrial enterprises. With the best intentions in the world one may try to introduce industry and attract – and keep – bullion but all the efforts in this direction will be of no avail and will have no permanent success in a country oppressed by political and religious despotism. This observation, based upon obvious facts, has escaped the notice of those economists who regard Spain as a glaring example of the uselessness of attempting to stimulate economic progress by restrictive measures. Poor dry soil produces a lean harvest but that does not mean that the seed is bad.

Spain and Portugal may be regarded as twins of the same age who have similar appearances, ideas, skills and prejudices. And they have made the same mistakes. They have also shared the same rise to fortune and they have suffered the same decline. Spain won the first prize by discovering the new world while the second fell to Portugal when she found a new passage to India round the Cape of Good Hope. The opening up of the new route to the East enabled Portugal to develop into a great trading nation and sea power while it dealt a fatal blow to the grandeur of Venice.

For centuries the Republic of Venice had brought together the ancient skills of Greece and Asia. Venice possessed industries of all kinds – above all the production of woollens, silks, glass-ware, and mirrors. For centuries Venice monopolised Europe's trade with the East Indies by way of Egypt. She had a firm base of operations on the Italian mainland and she seized the Morea,[1] Cyprus, Crete and several other islands (in the Mediterranean). After a struggle with the Republic of Genoa, which lasted for several hundred years, Venice succeeded in establishing her un-challenged maritime supremacy. But just as Genoa fell because its greatness had been founded upon the destruction of Pisa so Venice was punished because she preferred to dominate and to degrade her sister republics instead of forming an alliance with them as equals. When the Turks conquered Greece, the Venetians lost a consider-able part of their mainland territories as well as many islands. Portugal replaced Venice as far as trade with the East Indies was concerned. The Italian city states made the same mistakes as the Hanseatic League. They injured themselves by their rivalries. They failed to co-operate and to set up a united state. If they had united, their strength would have been quite sufficient to defeat the Turks and to seize most of the commerce that had been opened up by the great discoveries. The failure of the Venetians to secure a share in the trade with India round the Cape of Good Hope was due simply to the false political situation in which they had become involved. Since at the very time that they were fighting the Turks they had to keep a wary eye on their jealous rivals in Genoa, they could fight the Portuguese neither on the high seas nor in the East Indies, although they had more warships and more money at their disposal than the Portuguese. Like all declining powers Venice tried to cover up her

1. [A small part of Morea (Peloponnesus) was held by Venice in 1461-1540 and in 1684-1714.]

weakness by intrigues. But intrigues have little influence over the power of hard facts. Venice fell, never to rise again. Three hundred years ago this wealthy city was called the Queen of the Seas. Today Venice is merely a pile of stones in the middle of some marshes. It is no pleasant task to dissect decaying corpses. We shall confine ourselves to drawing attention to those factors in the commercial history of these countries in decline from which useful lessons can be drawn both for the present and the future.

In chapter 27 we showed in some detail how advantageous the Methuen Treaty had been for England and we pointed out that Adam Smith had passed a very different judgment on this agreement from that of statesmen, merchants, and manufacturers all over the world. Adam Smith endeavoured to show that this treaty benefitted Portugal and harmed England.

We shall not attempt to refute Adam Smith's arguments without, however, plunging into any theoretical controversy. We are concerned only with the very practical question as to whether commercial treaties of the Methuen type can be advantageous to a country like England which is striving towards the highest degree of industrialisation. It was a treaty of the Methuen type that England concluded with France in 1786. It was a treaty of this kind that Canning offered to Villèle and England would be glad to sign a similar treaty with any country that is unable to compete with her on equal terms.

Adam Smith writes in Chapter 16 of his fourth book that the Methuen Treaty was disadvantageous to England because England allowed Portuguese wine to be imported on payment of only one third of the duty charged on other wine. This placed Portugal in a privileged position. But England agreed that her woollen cloth should pay the same import duty in Portugal as that levied on other cloth. Consequently Portugal granted no special terms to England. But was not the English cloth industry far in advance of that of other countries? Was not England certain that she could sell more cloth in Portugal – without any privileges – than any other country? Were not the English, according to the *British Merchant*, able to defraud the Portuguese of half the duty on cloth? Were not the English, according to the same writer, able to buy Portuguese wine 15 per cent cheaper because of the rate of exchange? Did not the consumption of French and German wines, to which the English had been accustomed, cease on the day that the Methuen Treaty came into force? In fact the Portuguese enjoy a privilege in England that is only a privilege on paper while the English enjoy a privilege in Portugal which is a hard fact. A study of the true consequences of the Methuen Treaty provide the key to England's commercial policy from that day to this. The English have always been cosmopolitans and philanthropists in theory but always monopolists in practice.

Adam Smith did not deny that England enjoys the advantage of drawing large sums of money from Portugal in payment for her cloth. In his second argument against the Methuen Treaty he states that the English had no need to use the money received from the sale of cloth in Portugal to buy goods which they required from other countries. "But", wrote Adam Smith, "if those consumable goods were purchased directly with the produce of English industry, it would be more for the advantage of England than first to purchase with that produce the gold of Portugal, and afterwards to purchase with that gold those consumable goods. A direct foreign trade of consumption is always more advantageous than a round-about one; and to bring the same value of foreign goods to the home market, requires much smaller capital in the one way than in the other."[1]

If we did not have the greatest respect for the character of this distinguished writer – and for his wide knowledge and abilities – we would have to criticise him on this occasion for lack of judgment or for something worse. But as we are certain that Adam Smith had very great abilities we can only ascribe his casual and empty arguments to the weakness of human nature and to the zeal with which this eminent economist pursued the noble object which he always hoped to achieve – namely to convince humanity of the benefits to be derived from universal free trade.

Adam Smith's reasoning is as senseless as that of an economist who asserted that a baker would lose trade by selling bread for cash. If the baker were to ignore the customers to whom he sold bread for cash and were to go directly to the miller and exchange his bread for flour he would be doing business in one transaction instead of two. But even a person of only very limited abilities could answer such an argument. Since the miller does not need all the bread that the baker produces he can stay in business only if he can find people willing to pay cash for the surplus bread. Alternatively it could

1. [Adam Smith, *An Inquiry into the Nature and Causes of the Wealth of Nations* (1776) (Everyman edition, Vol. II, p. 46).]

be argued that although the miller would be prepared to sell his flour for cash he would refuse to exchange his flour for bread. That is exactly the position as far as England and Portugal are concerned. To make this quite clear we must examine the way in which commerce was conducted at the time of the Methuen Treaty. Portugal sent manufactured goods to the tropical regions of South America and received gold and silver in return. But since the Portuguese were too idle or too stupid to make manufactured goods themselves they had to use their gold and silver to buy the goods that they required in England or on the Continent. The countries receiving this gold and silver either minted it for use at home or they used it to trade in China or in the East Indies. England exported annually £500,000 to £1,000,000 to buy goods in China and India. Some of these goods from the East were consumed in England, while others were sold to various countries for gold and silver or for raw materials to be manufactured in English workshops. The demand for cloth was very small in Asia when compared with the demand in Portugal. And England's exports to India were valued at only about £160,000 a year at that time.

In the name of common sense we ask: Who would have purchased from England all the cloth that she exported to Portugal if the Portuguese had not bought the cloth or had bought it in France or Germany or had made it themselves in their own workshops? If this had happened England would have failed to sell her cloth in Portugal or in the Portuguese colonies. Her other customers were already buying as much English cloth as they required. The only sensible answer is: The English could not have produced the cloth which they had been selling to Portugal. They could not have obtained the gold and silver which they had formerly obtained from Portugal. They would not have had the gold and silver which they formerly sent to Asia. They would have bought fewer goods from India. They would also have bought fewer products from the Continent. And this massive decline in trade would have reduced England's productive powers. Portugal on the other hand – and those countries which supplied Portugal with manufactured goods – would have increased her productive powers. Most important of all there can be no question that England, without the Methuen Treaty, would never have extended her power in the East Indies.

Adam Smith's third argument is that the English would have secured the bullion that they required from some other source if they had failed to obtain it from Portugal. The gold and silver surplus to Portugal's needs would have been sent abroad and would then have reached England in one way or another. This argument is on similar lines to the second argument and it is self-contradictory. If the Portuguese had manufactured cloth themselves and had sent their surplus gold and silver to China and India it is not likely that England could have laid hands on it. The same thing would have happened if the Portuguese had bought the cloth they needed in Germany or in Flanders. In that case, as far as England was concerned, Portugal and her colonies would simply have ceased to exist and the English would not have produced a yard more cloth. The English could not have secured for themselves a grain more of gold or a pound more of spices from India than their limited exports would have permitted. This is proved by Germany's experience. Germany once had greater industries than England and even today has as fine intellectual and moral resources as any other country. It is proved also by the experience of all states which do not have a home market protected by commercial treaties of the Methuen type. And it would have been proved by the experience of England if her statesmen had followed Adam Smith's advice two hundred years ago.

It can be seen from Adam Smith's assessment of the Methuen Treaty how dangerous it would be for statesmen to act in conformity with an economic doctrine which is based upon a false cosmopolitanism and is supported only by evidence derived from the theory of value. Moreover the arguments employed by Adam Smith largely explain why the English honour his doctrine of foreign trade in theory but decline to put it into practice.

It would really be a master-stroke of England's policy to persuade other countries that commercial treaties of the Methuen type were disadvantageous to England and greatly to the advantage of other countries that signed them for Adam Smith has proved them with arguments supporting this point of view and they might think that they have good reason to accept his arguments.

We ask anyone who cannot understand the difference between national and cosmopolitan economists – and between the theories of productive powers and value – to turn his attention to Portugal and to England and to compare the economies of these two countries. I am sure that he can have no doubts as to which country is prosperous and which has lost its economic independence, is dead from an intellectual, commercial and industrial point of view, and is decadent, poverty stricken and weak.

———

CHAPTER THIRTY ONE

History of the Economic Policy of the United States of America[1]

FROM THE DAY that the American colonies were founded to the day that they became an independent state they were treated by the mother country as colonies to be cleared, planted, and exploited. In 1651 England imposed a heavy duty upon tobacco imported from Virginia. When the planters replied by exporting their tobacco to Holland, the English parliament passed an Act which provided that exports from the American colonies had to be sent first to an English port where the import duty had to be paid. This law remained in force until the revolt of the American colonies. When some industries were established in the colonies, despite the English monopoly, English ships were prohibited from handling American wool, yarn, or manufactured products.

In 1719 the House of Commons went still further. It declared that the development of industries in the American colonies en-

1. [For an earlier discussion of American economic policy see F. List, *Outlines of American Political Economy* ... (Philadelphia, 1827) and *Appendix to the Outlines of American Political Economy* ... (Philadelphia, 1827). The first pamphlet contained 8 letters to C.J. Ingersoll and the appendix contained 3 letters. The letters first appeared in the *National Gazette* (Philadelphia) between August 18 and November 27, 1827. The pamphlet and the appendix were reprinted in Margaret E. Hirst, *Life of Friedrich List* (1909) and in F. List, *Werke*, Vol. II, pp. 97-156. A twelfth letter (*National Gazette*, November 27, 1827) was not included in the two pamphlets of 1827 but has been printed in F. List, *Werke*, Vol. II, pp. 155-6.]

dangered their dependence upon the mother country and several laws were subsequently passed to check the growth of American industries. In 1750 Parliament actually denounced the very existence of American forges, foundries, ironworks on the coast, and several other colonial manufacturing enterprises as being "common nuisances" harmful to society. Sir Josiah Child and Dr Davenant both declared that the American colonies were the most harmful of all the overseas possessions because they were establishing their own industries (1670). It is to Adam Smith's credit that, in his famous book, he was the first to draw attention to the injustice of England's commercial policy with regard to the American colonies. The tyrannical attitude of England towards the commerce and industry of her colonies was one of the main reasons for the outbreak of the American war of independence.

There were two reasons why the war of independence fostered the growth of American industries. First, when the war broke out manufacturers were at once freed from all the restrictions previously imposed by the British government. Secondly, the establishment of new industrial enterprises was obviously necessary, profitable, and patriotic because the interruption to Anglo-American commerce stopped Americans from buying manufactured goods from England and from sending their products to England.

After the cessation of hostilities the loose links between the states of the Union were too weak to give adequate protection to the industry and commerce which had developed while trade with England had been interrupted during the war. Moreover the production of manufactured goods was seriously hampered because England continued to place import restrictions upon them. A country which had enjoyed the blessings of peace in wartime now suffered the inconveniences of war in time of peace. The slump in industry and trade was the main reason for the discontent in all the states of the Union in the early years of independence and this eventually brought about a revision of the constitution.

When the first Congress met in 1786 after the adoption of the new constitution nearly all the states – led by New York state and South Carolina – submitted petitions in favour of the protection of industry and shipping. On the day of the opening of Congress George Washington appeared dressed in a suit of homespun cloth and the official press declared that he had done so in order to set an example to all his countrymen and to show what should be done to place the independence and prosperity of the country on a sound footing.[1]

This Congress imposed import duties which were high enough to foster home industries in the early phase of their development. To promote the expansion of the mercantile marine Congress ordered that goods imported in American ships should pay 10 per cent less duty than goods imported in foreign vessels. The measures passed by Congress in 1786 were so effective that when he opened the Congress of 1791 the President was able to congratulate the country on the prosperous state of agriculture, industry, and commerce.

It soon became apparent, however, that the economy was being adversely affected by the restrictions which foreigners – particularly the English – had placed upon American trade. It was also obvious that the import duties originally imposed were too low to accomplish their object of adequately protecting American industry and shipping. Alexander Hamilton, the Secretary of the Treasury, was instructed to prepare a full report on American manufactures and he carried out this task in a very able manner. On the basis of Hamilton's report[2] James Madison proposed to the Congress of 1794 that import duties should be increased to protect the country's industry and shipping. This proposal was accepted. The main goods on which higher import duties were levied were woollens, calicos, and iron and steel products.

Although these import duties were still very moderate they were sufficient to enable all the eastern states of the United States to develop substantial industries. Later, however, owing to the rapid progress of England's industries, there were occasions on which certain branches of American manufacture – particularly such important industries as woollen and cotton cloths – suffered from

1. [List frequently repeated this story. It appears to refer not to the opening of the first Congress in 1786 but to Washington's inauguration of 1789. The *United States Gazette* (New York, May 6, 1789) reported: "The President of the United States on the day of his inauguration appeared dressed in a complete suit of homespun cloths. The cloth was of so fine a fabric and so handsomely finished, that it was universally mistaken for a foreign manufactured superfine cloth ... This circumstance must be considered as not only flattering to our manufacturers in particular, but interesting to our countrymen in general" (quoted in F. List, *Werke*, Vol. II, p. 184).]

2. [Alexander Hamilton, *Report of the Secretary of the Treasury of the United States on the Subject of Manufactures* ..., December 5, 1791 (second edition, 1824 edited by M. Carey). In a speech at a dinner given in his honour by the Pennsylvania Society for the Encouragement of Manufactures and the Mechanic Arts on November 3, 1827 List had referred to "Hamilton's celebrated work". See F. List, *Werke*, Vol. II, p. 168.]

English competition. But Congress showed no disposition to come to the aid of these industries so long as American farmers and merchants were prospering as a result of the wars that were raging in Europe. But the last war between England and the United States – and still more the peace that followed it – altered the situation completely. Both farming and foreign trade had been ruined during hostilities but all branches of industry had flourished. The peace led to a further decline in the fortunes of the merchants and the farmers and this at last led them to make common cause with the unfortunate industrialists, who were now suffering once more from English competition. For the second time the United States learned by bitter experience that a peace which sacrifices the industries of a nation to foreign competition is worse than a war.

The success of English competition coupled with England's refusal to admit American wheat and timber to her ports led to a widespread trade depression in the United States. The survival of American industry now became a national issue. The Congress of 1816 adopted a tariff which increased the import duties on English manufactured goods but eventually even this tariff was found to be too low to achieve its aim. The American factories did not revive and since the farmers could not sell their grain the price of agricultural produce fell more and more so that farmers and planters were faced with ruin.

In 1822 an attempt was made to alleviate the crisis by raising the tariff but the cotton planters – who play the same role in the United States as the winegrowers in France – had a vested interest in retaining a low tariff. In co-operation with the merchants interested in foreign commerce they were sufficiently powerful to override the interests of the nation as a whole.

By 1825 the number of bankruptcies among the wheat farmers had grown to such an alarming extent that Congress agreed to another increase in the tariff. As soon as information concerning the new duties reached England Huskisson went to work and took measures of retaliation against the Americans which gave English manufacturers the opportunity to compete successfully with the Americans in their home market.

England's retaliation placed the American manufacturers in an even worse position than before. Thinking that the new tariff would protect them in the home market they established many new enterprises only to find themselves faced with utter ruin from the moment that the new factories opened their doors. These circumstances, coupled with a renewed threat to American farming from the existing state of Anglo-American trade, eventually led to the adoption of the new tariff of 1828 – despite strong opposition from the cotton planters and the merchants engaged in foreign trade. This tariff at last gave American industry – particularly the cotton, woollen, and iron industries – adequate protection against foreign competition. It was the immediate cause of the prosperity that American industry has enjoyed from that day to this.

The tariff of 1828 was no more than a natural and necessary reply to England's commercial policy. England persistently refused to accept American wheat and timber in exchange for English manufactured goods. England would accept only those raw materials, such as cotton, which were indispensable to her own industry. As far as the United States was concerned this policy helped only the slave states which were, from an economic point of view, the most backward in the country. But England's policy ruined the most important, the most fertile, and the most prosperous states in the Union. Every year the profits from their economic activities were counterbalanced by the loss of 500,000 of their best farm workers who migrated to the wilderness in the West. Huskisson fully appreciated the situation. It is common knowledge that the British ambassador in Washington frequently warned his government of the consequences that would follow from the exclusion of American products from the English market. Had Huskisson really been a leading cosmopolitan – as the doctrinaire economists on the Continent would have us believe – he would have taken the opportunity afforded by the imposition of the new American tariff to make it clear to the English nobility that the imposition of the new American tariff was a glorious consequence of their precious Corn Laws. He would have told them that only the abolition of these senseless laws would enable English industry to recover at any rate a part of the American market, which they now risked losing altogether. But what did Huskisson do? He railed against the Americans like a cardsharper whose slight of hand has been exposed. He made reckless assertions that every American who worked on the land knew to be palpably false. He made threats against the Americans that he had no means of carrying out. In short he made a complete fool of himself. Huskisson declared that the exports of the United States to England amounted to half her total exports but that England's exports to the United States amounted to only one sixth of her total exports. From this he concluded that the Americans were more in England's power than England was at the mercy of the United States. This superficial argument may sound plausible but every American farmer knows perfectly well the true nature of Anglo-American trade. He knows that the exports of the United States to England are all raw materials that England cannot do without and that the value of these products is increased tenfold in the manufacturing process. On the other hand he also knows that all England's exports to the United States are manufactured goods which the United States can very well do without since she can either make such goods herself or she can buy them from France or Germany. Consequently England is in the power of the United States in two ways. Huskisson boasted of the great increase in the imports of American cotton to England in recent years. That is true but it should be appreciated that this increase took place in a manner advantageous to England and harmful to the United States. This was because the output of raw cotton was continually expanding faster than the demands of the market. Consider the significance of the following facts. In 1816 the Americans sold 81 million lbs of cotton for 24 million dollars while in 1826 they sold 204 lbs for only 25 million dollars. The Americans had sold three times as much cotton in 1826 as compared with 1816 but the revenue earned from the cotton had risen by only one twentyfifth. In these circumstances the English landlords could hardly take Huskisson's arguments very seriously. Finally Huskisson threatened to restrict the imports of American cotton. Can one really believe what he says? I doubt it. If Huskisson really meant what he said it would cast genuine doubts upon his intellectual capacity, upon his practical knowledge, and upon his political integrity. Did he really imagine that the Americans were so simple as to be cowed by his empty threats? It is certain that the Americans were perfectly well aware of the following facts: (1) that cotton from India is poor in quality, (2) that India, Brazil, and Egypt can only expand their output of cotton very slowly, and (3) that so long as England cannot get the cotton she needs from countries other than the United States the imposition of a high import duty upon raw cotton would benefit only the cotton industry on the Continent and would damage the English cotton industry. For obvious reasons such a policy would encourage the development of the manufacture of cotton goods in the United States and this would soon become the most important cotton industry in the world.

Another of Huskisson's threats ran counter to the most ordinary common sense. He actually suggested that by smuggling goods across the Canadian frontier the English could avoid the damage to their trade which would probably be caused by the American tariff. Though England does not generally fear retaliation she would certainly avoid it in that part of the world.

Huskisson obviously erred in his assessment of the Americans and their economy just as Canning erred in his assessment of France and the French. The age of Methuen treaties has passed away and free trade economists cannot for ever hope to throw dust in people's eyes. Today it is deeds that count, not words. The time has passed when it was possible to persuade a nation to adopt a particular commercial policy by gaining the ear of a few ministers of state. Today there are so many journalists writing for so many newspapers, there are so many readers of newspapers, and there are so many people capable of thinking for themselves that it needs more than long-winded debates in parliament and low diplomatic tricks to gain popular support for a commercial treaty. Nowadays the truth must be told to gain the support of the people for a trade agreement and it is essential that they should be convinced that the terms will be favourable to both parties.

We have considered it necessary to discuss the policy of Canning and Huskisson both in this chapter and in other parts of our treatise because for many years we have marvelled at the way in which their political activities have been misunderstood by continental philosophers and politicians. The views of politicians have obviously been influenced by the fact that these two ministers were Whigs who were bitterly attacked by the Tories. The liberals on the Continent believed that the Whigs were their friends and that Canning and Huskisson were flesh of their flesh.

Heavens above! An English Whig is always an Englishman. And any Englishman – especially if he is the leader of his country – would never be a cosmopolitan except in the sense that the term was once applied to the Hansards, the Venetians, and the Dutch. "I fear the Greeks even when they bring gifts."

CHAPTER THIRTY TWO

History of Russia's Economic Policy

SINCE THE RULERS of Russia had been instructed in the doctrine of free trade by (their tutor) Heinrich Storch[1] it is not surprising that as soon as the Continental System was abolished and general peace was restored, the Russian Empire should have lost no time in enjoying the blessings of free trade. The Russian tariff of 1819[2] was, as far as possible, true to the principles of free trade and the results were soon evident. Russia was flooded with foreign goods, the home market was ruined, and most of the country's bullion was drained away to foreign countries. If anything was needed to render the doctrinaire theory of free trade even more ridiculous it was the fact that all this happened at the very time when Great Britain was imposing restrictions on the import of Russia's wheat and of most of her raw materials. Even when the depression in Russia reached its climax the government persisted in the policy of free trade for some time because the doctrinaire economists assured the Czar that the disastrous consequences of free trade would be only temporary in duration and would undoubtedly be followed by better times. The Czar waited for four years for the fulfilment of the prophecy of the free traders.

Eventually the distress in Russia became so great that serious consequences were feared. Even Napoleon's invasion had not brought such disasters to the country as the much vaunted policy of free trade. The Czar decided to reverse his economic policy but so great was the influence of the supporters of free trade that even the

1. [See H. Storch, *Cours d'économie politique ou exposition des principes qui déterminent la prospérité des nations: ouvrage qui a servi à l'instruction de Leurs Altesses impériales, les Grands-Ducs Nicolas et Michel* (6 vols, St Petersburg, 1815 and 4 vols, Paris, 1824). This book was published at the expense of Czar Alexander I. Storch was born in Riga in 1766 and died in 1835. According to G. von Schulze-Gaevernitz, *Volkswirtschaftliche Studien zu Russland* (1899), p. 244 the Russian tariff of 1819 was inspired by the Prussian (Maassen) tariff of the previous year and was only "a temporary deviation" from the normal Russian fiscal policy of prohibitions and high import duties.]
2. [The Russian tariff was dated November 22, 1819. List wrote "1818" in error.]

autocratic government considered it prudent to justify its action by a public statement. In a circular dispatch of March 22, 1822 Count Nesselrode wrote: "The landowners have no market for their produce, the workshops are completely ruined, our precious metals have been exported, and the most solid mercantile houses face bankruptcy."

Since those days Russia has reversed her fiscal policy and we no longer hear of any distress in that country. In fact it is said that agriculture, industry, and commerce are now enjoying a new period of prosperity. Russia, however, is obviously not yet ready for the adoption of a fully fledged policy of protection.

CHAPTER THIRTY THREE

The Spirit of different Economic Doctrines in Relation to Tariff Laws

THE TWO FUNDAMENTAL principles of the mercantile system were that a country can prosper only at the expense of another country and that national wealth consists solely of precious metals. It followed that a nation should try to secure as much money as possible from foreign states and should take steps to ensure that it stayed within its own frontiers. This policy was derived from the narrow myopic vision of merchants and it was put into practice by imposing a tariff to restrict the export of precious metals as much as possible.

It would be a mistake to confuse the "mercantile system" with the "manufacturing system" and to condemn both in the same breath. The "manufacturing system" was described by certain writers before Colbert's day. It was first practised by the English government and was later copied by Colbert. The Italians called this system "Colbertism" and they differentiated between the "mercantile system" and the "manufacturing system".

Supporters of the "manufacturing system" do not suggest that a country can prosper only at the expense of another country. Their object is to enrich all the citizens in a country – manufacturers, farmers, and merchants trading at home and abroad. The "manufacturing system" seeks to establish and to foster industry and the "productive powers" of the nation. In practice it has invariably achieved its aims, provided that it has been supported by suitable social, moral, and political institutions and provided that adequate natural resources are available. Supporters of the "manufacturing system" often imposed import duties to protect native industry from foreign competition in the home market. But when they went so far as to restrict the export of agricultural produce and raw materials in the interest of the industrialists they injured those who made their living on the land and they flouted all cosmopolitan principles. The "manufacturing system" had become narrowly nationalistic and the outlook of its supporters had become far too restricted.

The "agricultural system" – the doctrines advocated by the Physiocrats – was simply a reaction against the "mercantile system" and the "manufacturing system". In exposing the errors of the earlier theories the Physiocrats went to the other extreme and championed an opposite doctrine which virtually amounted to pure cosmopolitanism. They wanted to secure prosperity for the whole human race but in trying to attain their aims they failed to appreciate – indeed they entirely ignored – the particular interests of various nations. Confused by the weaknesses and limitations of the "manufacturing system", the Physiocrats thought that economic expansion could be promoted only by establishing complete free trade throughout the world. They laid down *a priori* principles and only later began to look for evidence to prove that they were correct. They saw that in the very nature of things the existence of nation-states prevented the fulfilment of their aims. An examination of Colbert's achievements convinced them that in the modern world – in which the human race is divided into nations – the establishment and development of industries can be fostered only by the imposition of tariffs. But as their outlook was completely cosmopolitan they turned a blind eye to the very existence of national tariffs. The "agricultural system" of the Physiocrats, though founded upon quicksands, was the first economic doctrine to recognise fully the significance of agriculture and to bring into the limelight the interests of the whole human race, which the mercantilists had failed to recognise.

We now come to the "cosmopolitan system". We can think of no better name for the doctrines advocated by Adam Smith and J. B. Say. The supporters of these doctrines recognise that the arguments of the Physiocrats are untenable and they have restored industry to its rightful place in the economy. And they have shown that industry is mainly responsible for the development of a prosperous agriculture.

Blinded by the cosmopolitan doctrine of free trade the supporters of the "cosmopolitan system" have taken the wrong road to achieve their purpose. They have fallen into the same trap as the Physiocrats by first asserting a principle and then looking for evidence to support it. They have not appreciated the significance of the fact that humanity is divided into various nations, each with its own individuality. They have failed to recognise the existence of a problem posed by nature itself – namely how to unite the "productive powers" of all individuals so that they can pursue a common goal to their mutual advantage. Since such unwelcome facts are incompatible with the "cosmopolitan principle" they have simply been ignored. The supporters of the "cosmopolitan principle" have silently averted their eyes from the obvious fact that nations exist and they have simply imagined the existence of a world republic.

At the same time they have also been forced to ignore wars and the consequences of wars or at any rate they have had to postulate the absence of such disagreeable events. They regard tariffs as the result of a mistaken fiscal policy whereas they are really brought about by the division of mankind into independent sovereign states. Supporters of the cosmopolitan doctrine are treading a path that ignores reality and they pretend that what in fact exists is not there at all. Consequently all their conclusions are absolutely worthless in practice. On the other hand practical men have to accept the fact that national rivalries and international conflicts do exist and they have to cope with the consequences of this state of affairs. Moreover the "cosmopolitan system" is a purely materialistic conception which fails to take account of the human spirit – and the human power – that lie behind material things. At best the "cosmopolitan system" lays far greater stress upon material objects than upon the creative power which makes possible the production of material goods. The supporters of the "cosmopolitan system" make this mistake – just as they made the fundamental mistake which we have already mentioned – because they lay down *a priori* doctrines and then try to prove them.[1] They consider it axiomatic that all production depends upon labour and upon the value of material things. But as soon as they attempt to develop and to elucidate these principles in conformity with what happens in the real world it becomes crystal clear that their doctrines can be applied only to material goods that have already been produced and cannot be applied to productive powers which obey entirely different laws.

This has led the supporters of the "cosmopolitan system" to reach certain erroneous conclusions. They have concluded that since goods can be bought only in exchange for other goods, the exchange of products by foreign trade is always desirable. In their opinion it follows that it is always foolish to attempt to regulate by law what a country produces. They argue that if the output of a particular commodity is diverted into channels different from those intended by nature – because of restrictions imposed by another country – there is nothing that can be done to remedy the injury. They consider that any attempt at retaliation would only make matters worse by adding a second injury to the first. They believe that as far as foreign trade is concerned, nations show the greatest wisdom when they buy in the cheapest market and then allow nature to take its course.

Those who argue in this way completely fail to recognise that it is only step by step that nations are able to secure the development of their agriculture to a high standard of efficiency. They forget that the basic foundations for the maintenance and future development of manufacturing power are progress in agriculture, culture, power, and independence. They forget that this manufacturing power can-not develop in relatively backward countries under conditions of free competition, particularly when that competition comes from a highly industrialised country. They forget that a nation begins to establish industries with a view to developments that will occur not just in a few years but in hundreds – even thousands – of years in the future. In fact these developments will take place throughout the whole life of the nation. They forget that from this point of view the theory of value does not come into the picture at all; that

1. [List's note] Droz (*Econ. polit.*, introduction vi) vigorously criticises those who do not take the trouble to distinguish between what is known and what is not known – and this is the only way to arrive at the truth. [The full reference is Joseph Droz, *Économie politique ou principes de la science des riches* (Paris, 1829).]

a tariff is the only way to establish industries so that they eventually reach a high standard of efficiency; that nations develop great industries because they possess the necessary natural resources and intellectual qualities. Above all they forget that this is the certain means by which mankind will eventually achieve the goal of universal free trade. This can never be achieved if one ignores the natural course of human development.

By ignoring all these considerations the supporters of the "cosmopolitan system" inevitably become involved in endless contradictions and they have put forward arguments which are contrary to the course of nature. They acknowledge the importance of industry and they agree that there can be no progress, no culture, and no agriculture without it. Yet they vociferously reject the only means by which the expansion of industry can be attained. Unable to deny that all industrialised states have become rich and powerful, they argue that this has happened in spite of – and not because of – their tariffs. In one chapter they praise poor Colbert, while in the next they attack him.[1] They feel that they must denounce tariffs although tariffs are simply a method by which a state reserves trade for itself. They have to argue that tariffs protect industry at the expense of agriculture although in fact it is agriculture that gains most from tariffs (on manufactured goods). They have to assert that a tariff robs agriculture of capital although in fact industry generally uses only resources and powers which, in a purely rural society, lie dormant and are of no use. They have even found it expedient to criticise and to deprecate commercial treaties which are in fact the only way by which freedom of trade can be secured. Indeed it is precisely those commercial agreements which are in closest accord with the "cosmopolitan system" which have failed completely to produce the results prophesied by the free traders.

1. [List's note] Say states (P.I., p.294 of his *Traité*): "The stimulus which Colbert gave to manufactures placed a burden upon agriculture". On page 279 of the same volume, however, he observes: "Perhaps they (the silk and cloth industries) benefitted from the stimulus given to them by Colbert." On page 275 he states: "If an industry is profitable it needs no stimulus and if there is no likelihood of a profit there is no point in fostering the industry" and then in the same chapter on page 275 he observes: "It would perhaps be right to stimulate some industries which may prosper in the future". On page 268 in the same chapter Say states: "Commercial treaties are valuable only if they protect an industry – and the capital invested in it – which has developed on wrong lines owing to bad laws". Finally Say states (P.II, p.404) that "agriculture will always be in a wretched and depressed state unless a country has flourishing towns and prosperous industries". There are indeed many contradictions here.

The following argument illustrates in a striking fashion how blind to reality are the supporters of the "cosmopolitan system". They assert that nature ordains that people should trade according to the principle of freedom of commerce. They proclaim that nature utterly rejects restrictions on commerce because she has endowed different peoples with different resources and the ability to produce different products. They argue that it would be flying in the face of reason to try to make the northern countries grow the fruits of the southern countries. This argument is all very fine but we have already shown in chapter 17 that it applies only to agricultural products. As far as the output of manufactured goods is concerned it is obvious that the major states in the temperate zone – if they possess the necessary moral qualities and the necessary political and cultural institutions – are all equally capable of establishing great industries. Scholars of the calibre of Adam Smith and Say would undoubtedly have appreciated this distinction had they not been prejudiced by a principle which they feel that they must defend at all costs.

The best proof of the errors and weaknesses of the "cosmopolitan system" is the inability of its supporters to explain how the world republic of the future is to achieve universal free trade. And they have never made the smallest efforts to achieve this goal in practice.[1]

Adam Smith has been highly praised for teaching that a nation's wealth consists not merely of precious metals but of all kinds of products that have exchange-value. This would indeed be a highly significant observation but for the fact that something even more significant than material objects also deserves attention. This is the human factor – the will and the ability to produce goods. Those who lose the will to produce decline into a state of weakness, poverty, and distress, however much wealth they may possess in terms of material products. We have already illustrated the truth of this statement by discussing the fall of Venice, the Hanseatic League, Spain, and Portugal. It has also been claimed that Adam Smith showed that labour was the only real source of national wealth. The

1. [List's note] Say contradicts himself when he writes: "Perhaps a government would be well advised to foster certain types of industrial production. Losses might be sustained at first, but after a few years valuable benefits would result from such a course of action". This "perhaps" completely contradicts Say's rejection of state aid to industry. And does he not admit that an industry will prosper only after many years have passed – and not just in a few years? Does a nation exist for only a few years?

fact that there is virtually no truth in this narrow, limited definition of the origin of wealth is, in itself, a proof of the utter inadequacy and weakness of the entire "cosmopolitan system". Adam Smith might just as well have argued that human hands and feet are the source of all wealth. It would be just as impossible to derive any sensible principles or conclusions from such a statement.

It is meaningless to claim that the work people do is the origin and the cause of wealth. Is there no difference between the work performed on a steamship by the boy who handles the rudder and by the engineer? The physical labour of the boy at the rudder may be ten times heavier than that of the engineer but the work performed by the engineer is a thousand times more important than that of the boy. Leaving on one side the power of machinery one might point to the difference in output of the physical labour of an Englishman and some undernourished Indian. One might compare the work of two farmers, one of whom is far away from any industrial towns where he might have commercial contacts, while the other is in close touch with a number of different manufacturers. Again there is a significant difference between the output of demoralised superstitious slaves and that of free, enlightened, cultured, and intelligent workers.

To obtain a clear and accurate picture of productive powers – and of the means by which those powers can be developed and protected – it is necessary to ask the question: If work produces wealth, what produces work? What makes men set their hands and feet in motion to make something? What contributes to the success of their efforts? We always find that there is some inner urge which sets the human body in motion. The more that a man appreciates that he must provide for his own future, and that of his dependants, the greater will be his efforts and the more work will he perform. The more that a man has been accustomed to work from his earliest days, the more that his education has awakened his latent powers, the more that he follows the good example of his parents and teachers, the less likely will it be that he will allow himself to be diverted from his tasks by erroneous or superstitious views. Such a man will find that his technical skill and his zeal for work will increase as time goes by and consequently his output will increase. Christianity, monogamy, and freedom are more likely to foster the development of productive powers than Mohammedanism, polygamy, and servitude or a very limited amount of freedom. And there are even significant differences between the productive powers of the adherents of various Christian churches.

Nature supplements and increases men's productive powers and output by the power of water, wind, animals, and steam. But men can use these natural powers to establish advanced types of workshops and factories only after they have made the requisite intellectual progress. They must be enlightened and well educated and they should have a good knowledge of science as well as high standards of technical skill. Consequently the workers in an advanced country have a much greater output than workers in a backward country.

It follows that certain conditions must be fulfilled before men's productive powers, and their intellectual and physical labours, can be successfully applied to the production of material goods that have an exchange value. There must be good laws, effectively enforced. Persons and property must enjoy the maximum security. The people must have high moral and religious standards so that superstition, prejudice, and vice can be rooted out. There must be a good system of education. Science and the arts must be zealously fostered. Workshops and factories must receive adequate protection. There should be a harmonious balance between all branches of production. In general the whole national economy should be stimulated. The government should safeguard economic prosperity at home and should protect the country from foreign aggressors. Moreover the labours of those who promote the expansion of productive powers are just as productive as those who actually make goods that have an exchange-value.

Our opponents might argue that the principle we have advanced could be interpreted as meaning that economic prosperity is related to the number of lawyers, parsons, soldiers, teachers, and scholars who are working in a country. It is easy to refute this sophism. Intellectual production and brainwork – like manual labour and the production of material goods – cannot be measured by counting the number of individuals concerned. Two hundred workers – given the necessary power driven machinery – can make as many garments as 1,000 men who are working without these aids to production. In this case 1,000 workers on their own produce less than 200 workers with power-driven machines. Similarly 1,000 teachers and parsons, who pursue their vocations zealously, can produce more intellectual powers than 100,000 less dedicated men.

Adam Smith regarded the physical labour which produces goods having exchange-value as the sole source of wealth and he failed to examine the origins of the powers that enable this work to be done. From this failure came his serious mistake of ignoring the intellectual resources that lie behind the creation of productive powers. Had Adam Smith examined these intellectual resources he must surely have recognised the significance of industrial power for all the other economic activities carried on in a country and he would not have fallen into the error of judging foreign trade by the theory of exchange-value.

J.B. Say appreciated Adam Smith's error and replaced the word "labour", which Adam Smith used, by "industrious classes" but this also has too narrow and limited a meaning. We can prove that Say failed to recognise – or at least failed to recognise fully – the existence of productive powers by drawing attention to the following facts: (1) Say takes exactly the same view of commercial and trading restrictions as Adam Smith, (2) Say does not appreciate that a native industry is absolutely essential to the development of a nation's culture, independence, and power, and for the fullest expansion of agriculture, (3) Say completely fails to understand the influence of the political and social state of a country upon its economic development. For these reasons Say makes the same mistakes as his predecessors.

The doctrine of productive powers has become widely known through the comprehensive and learned writings of Chaptal, Charles Dupin, and Droz. These scholars have deepened our knowledge of the true nature of economics. Chaptal has limited his researches to showing how the national wealth of France has increased as the result of a policy of fostering home industry and foreign commerce. Dupin has brought together statistics illustrating not only what Say calls "industry" but also on the moral condition, the intellectual capacity, the educational facilities, and the social and political institutions of France. He has made a thorough, detailed, comprehensive, and systematic examination of the way in which all France's productive powers have been applied in practice. The profundity of his researches, the clarity of his thinking, and the completeness of his survey – rather than his criticism of Adam Smith – have brilliantly illuminated the gross inadequacy of the "cosmopolitan system". Droz has written a remarkably lucid criticism of the "cosmopolitan system" of Adam Smith and Say and has concluded his book with an excellent, detailed and well written chapter in which he compared the "cosmopolitan system" with the doctrine of productive powers. Had he expanded this chapter he might have formulated a new doctrine which would be based firmly upon what happens in the real world.

In previous chapters we have shown how the English have paid homage to a doctrine that has enabled their country to become the mistress of the world and to ensure her supremacy in the future. English economists have denounced the opposition of practical men in other countries to their theories as short-sighted and narrow minded. This is quite natural.[1] In England economic theory and practice go hand in hand and even the erroneous aspects of the doctrine of free trade have proved to be to England's advantage.

German economists have also paid homage to the doctrine of free trade and still do so. This too is understandable. Some German economists have actually resurrected the theories of the Physiocrats from the dusty tomes in which they first appeared. So far it has been impossible for Germany to adopt a national commercial system because the country is divided into a number of small states. German intellectuals naturally welcomed the doctrine of free trade and they hoped that its adoption would bring prosperity to their country. It is perfectly understandable that they should have embraced the theories of the "cosmopolitan system". It is quite natural that a weak country, oppressed by a powerful neighbour, should seek refuge in a doctrine based upon the principles of justice and morality.

There are, however, countries which – although their industries are quite well developed – have suffered from the ruthless economic policy of a still more advanced industrial nation. It is really astonishing that there are people in such countries who are prepared to defend and to support the "cosmopolitan system". The practical results of the acceptance of this system by the countries in question would be a decline in their wealth, power, and culture as well as oppression on the part of the rival industrially advanced nation. Such an attitude is surely contrary to common sense. Only intellectual blindness and crass egotism can explain the behaviour of such supporters of the "cosmopolitan system".

Doctrinaire economists declare that any failure to accept England's industrial supremacy would harm the whole world. They

1. [List's note] Montesquieu makes a penetrating observation on England's policy when he quotes Cicero – Nolo eundem populum imperatorem et portatorem esse.

consider that England has made such striking industrial progress and has extended her economic influence so far afield that humanity would make more progress if things were left as they are than if nations which can be compared with England in culture and power should try to catch up with her from an industrial point of view by adopting restrictive commercial practices.

We would be prepared to agree with these economists if it were true that the nations concerned had decided to seek salvation under the supremacy of England and were prepared to surrender their rights as sovereign states. In fact it is hardly to be expected that nations would do this even if one could convince them that England is really greatly superior to all other countries. If the existence of such an attitude cannot be proved – and it is certainly not universally held – then we must expect the French, Americans, Belgians, and other peoples to cherish the hope that they can promote their industrial, social, and political development by the same methods as those employed by the English. In that case no mere doctrine can be expected to prevent a country from adopting such a policy. Other countries will always regard as ridiculous the notion that England should always be supreme and that their own economic advance should for ever be retarded to benefit the progress of humanity. They believe that the existing state of affairs has arisen simply because England – exceptionally favoured by nature and by chance – has enjoyed a 30 to 50 year head start over her rivals. They believe that humanity may make rather slower progress because of their protective commercial policies but they consider that such progress will be more balanced than would otherwise be the case. The protection of national industries will enable states to preserve their freedom. The establishment of a universal republic will be much more likely if all the civilised countries in the world – followed in due course by countries which are at present relatively backward – were making uniform economic progress. This would be much better than a situation in which one country dominated all others in industrial and commercial power, because in that case a world trading monopoly and a universal despotism would have been established.

CHAPTER THIRTY FOUR

The Natural System of Political Economy[1]

WE HAVE GIVEN the name "Natural System" to the economic doctrine that we have put forward in this treatise. We have not made any *a priori* assertions and then attempted to prove them. We have arrived at our conclusions by proving the truth of principles derived from what actually happens in the real world. We are not numbered among those who deny that nations have individual characteristics and special interests. We have not ignored the fact that these interests give rise to special relationships between them. For our part we favour the eventual unification of all the peoples in the world on the basis of the existence of different nations. We regard both free trade and a universal republic as the natural consequence of the harmonious and uniform development of the political and social institutions of all countries.

Doctrinaire economists cannot accuse us of defending the policy of protection on the ground that we propose – as the mercantilists proposed – to secure wealth for a nation at the expense of other countries. Nor do we propose to keep our gold and silver within the frontiers of our own country, to attract precious metals from other states, and to secure a favourable balance of trade. Our opponents cannot accuse us of failing – as the supporters of the "manufacturing system" have failed – to appreciate that nature has favoured some countries with regard to certain products and other countries with regard to other products. We advocate the greatest possible measure of freedom of commerce as far as foodstuffs and raw materials are concerned. Our opponents cannot accuse us of wishing to keep the world divided for ever into different nations which are continually hostile to one another. We regard nationalism as

1. [List did not give his treatise a title but the heading which he gave to Chapter 34 justifies the use of the title *The Natural System of Political Economy*]

simply one particular stage of human development, which will one day be replaced by cosmopolitanism. Our opponents cannot accuse us of failing to appreciate the great merits of the "cosmopolitan system" since we have accepted its theory of value. We have merely argued that there is also a theory of productive powers and that when questions of international trade are under discussion the theory of value should be regarded as subordinate to the theory of productive powers. Our critics cannot accuse us of failing to appreciate the significance of Adam Smith's book although we have rejected his view that labour is the origin of wealth. J.B. Say has shown that Adam Smith's definition of "labour" is much too narrow. We believe that we have shown that the conception of "industrious classes" that Say puts in place of Adam Smith's "labour" is also a very narrow definition which interprets productive powers in far too materialistic a fashion.

Practical men, for their part, cannot accuse us of failing to appreciate that every nation has its own particular problems and interests. They cannot allege that we pretend that humanity is in a situation that does not exist at present although it may exist one day. They cannot suggest that we have tried to support our conclusions with arguments that defy common sense and universal experience. They must recognise that we have advanced theoretical arguments in favour of more than half of their demands for tariff protection. The only difference of opinion between ourselves and the practical men is that they wish to stimulate agriculture by the imposition of import duties and that they propose that all tariffs should last for ever.

We call our doctrines the "Natural System" because we believe that they enable us to draw attention to the mistakes and contradictions of the supporters of the "cosmopolitan system" and that we have been able to show how a harmonious relationship can be established between economic theory and economic practice.

CHAPTER THIRTY FIVE

The Question posed by the Academy

WE HAVE now completed our treatise which answers the question:
"If a country proposes to introduce free trade or to modify its
tariff, what factors should it take into account so as to reconcile
in the fairest manner the interests of producers with those of consumers?"

A distinction should be made between countries which have
reached different stages of economic development.

1. We consider first a country which is retarded with regard
to its cultural, moral, social, and political development. It has
no independent prosperous middle class. Its land, capital, and
technical knowledge are in the hands of a small privileged class.
Agriculture is relatively backward and those who work on the land
have little technical knowledge. To promote the rapid economic
expansion of such a country it will be necessary to encourage the
import of manufactured goods – assuming of course that the country
supplying these goods does not impose import duties or prohibitions upon the import of foodstuffs and raw materials in exchange.
In these circumstances the agrarian country should trade with those
industrialised countries offering the best terms and it should reserve
the right to extend its commerce in the future to any other industrialised country which is prepared to do business on similar terms.

2. Secondly, we will examine the position of a country which has
all the necessary cultural qualifications for future industrial progress, but has only a small territory and cannot expect to be able to
set up manufactures on a substantial scale because it lacks both
adequate natural resources and a large enough home market. Such
a country should endeavour to expand its markets either by entering
into a customs union or by concluding commercial treaties with
other countries.

3. Thirdly, we will deal with a country in which all the conditions
for future industrial expansion are satisfied. When considering such

a country – one which has reached the first stage of industrialisation – it is necessary to know

(a) if the country already operates a system of prohibitions or high import duties. If this is the case the rates of the duties should gradually be lowered until protection is afforded only to those branches of manufacture which appear to stand a good chance of being profitable at some time in the future.

(b) if the country has no protective tariff but proposes to establish one. In this case the best policy to adopt would be gradually to protect and to foster the development of those branches of manufacture which appear likely to be successful in the future.

4. We shall now consider a country in which all the conditions for future industrialisation have been satisfied. This is a country which is capable of progressing to the most advanced stage of industrialisation. If such a country has already fully developed its productive powers by means of a prohibitive system, it should be prepared to change gradually to a protective system.

5. Finally, we will consider an industrialised country in which manufactures have developed to such an extent that – even if it adopts a policy of free trade – it is in a position to compete successfully with any other country. Such a country should gradually reduce its import duties so as to allow foreign manufactured goods to come on to the home market to compete with native products.

In Chapter 12 to 26 we have discussed the desirability of complete freedom of trade in all agricultural products; the need to be prepared to change from one fiscal system to another; the circumstances under which a country should protect native industries, as well as various aspects of foreign competition.

APOLOGY

The author refers his readers to the long note on page 17.[1] The hour has struck when he has to deliver the manuscript of his treatise to the Academy. He has not had sufficient time either to correct numerous slips made by the copyist or to add a number of notes and references.

[I.e. page 17 of List's manuscript (Chapter 4). This note is printed below as an appendix.]

List's Note to Chapter 4[1]

THE STEEL PEN with which I have written both the rough copy and the final version of this treatise, and the fine paper on which it has been written may serve as an excellent example to illustrate clearly and simply the differences between the doctrines of exchange-value and productive powers.

At first I thought that it would be wasteful to use fine paper for the rough copy as well as for the final version but then I realised that my steel pen wrote much better on fine paper than on paper of poorer quality. Moreover the steel pen makes a noise when I write on paper of poor quality and this disturbs my train of thought. So I made a calculation. To live by my pen as an author I must earn 40 francs a day. The treatise has taken me 40 days to write, representing an earning power of 1,600 francs. Had I lost time by sharpening my pen or by writing more slowly and had I been disturbed by the noise caused by writing on poor paper I might have taken 70 days to write the treatise at a loss to my earning power of 2,800 francs. Under the most favourable circumstances I might not have gained an "exchange-value".[2]

By using better tools I have been able to reduce my costs to 1,600 francs. The better pens and the finer paper have cost 40 francs at the most so I have made a net saving of 1,560 francs. This calculation is based upon the theory of value. But a calculation based upon the theory of productive powers would give a different result. In this case the gain by using better pens and finer paper is much greater. Assuming that my annual output of new ideas exercises some influence upon the productive powers of people like myself – which is not very likely – I would be able to double my influence over the

1. [List wrote this long note to Chapter 4 after his manuscript had been completed. It is printed at the end of the book as an appendix. Although List purports to discuss the theories of value and productive powers examined in Chapter 4, the note is really an apology for having written the treatise in a very short time.]
2. [I.e. List might not win the prize offered by the Academy.]

general public. But if this treatise should possess any intellectual merit it would be due entirely to the speed of its composition. For over 20 years I have been making observations and I have been thinking about what I discuss in my manuscript but it has taken me only 40 days to plan the enterprise, to read the necessary books, to make the necessary notes, and to write down my views and criticisms. In addition I have had to supervise the making of a fair copy. To complete my task in time I could not wait until the whole of the original rough copy was finished before starting on the fair copy, although this would have been desirable when composing a treatise of this length. I have had to hand my rough draft to the copyist as soon as it was written. At the same time I was afraid that I might have dealt with some aspects of the problem too fully or not fully enough. In the first case there was a danger of submitting an ill-digested treatise. In the second case there was a danger that the adjudicators – who set such high standards for themselves – might consider that my work had fallen below the standard that they had a right to expect. In either case I would have failed to achieve my aim which is to be worthy of the votes and the support of the learned body which takes the first place in the world in every branch of knowledge to which it has turned its attention. It is a body which has the power to confer the greatest distinction or to deliver the most damning criticism on any literary project.

Were my treatise so imperfect or so incomplete as to merit my own condemnation I would not have submitted it to the Academy. Since I mistrust my own abilities when my initial efforts have been unsuccessful, I would probably have left the work unfinished and I would have troubled myself no more about it. If, despite all the unfavourable circumstances connected with its composition, I have nevertheless been able to produce something worth while, this has been due to the increase in my productive powers brought about by my good pens and my fine paper. At the same time this is also a striking proof of the possible harmful consequences of prohibitions since both pens and paper have been made in England.

I must explain why I have had so short a time in which to write my treatise. I was under the impression – by what mischance I do not know – that the adjudication of the essays answering the Academy's question had already taken place. It was only two months ago that I learned that this was not the case. I could not start work on the manuscript for a fortnight owing to other literary commitments.

I hesitate to explain the particular circumstances of the composition of the manuscript but I think that I should do so in the hope of securing the indulgence of the adjudicators. I have not had time either to check my first rough draft or my fair copy. The style of the composition will inevitably bear witness to my haste. The final copy has been written by two persons[1] and I am unable to assess the competence of one of them. Even as I write this note (on the last day before the expiry of the extended time limit for submitting the treatise) I do not know if I can find time to number the chapters and the notes and to fill in any gaps left by the copyist because he has not been able to read what I have so hurriedly written.

A candidate for an Academy award may presume to hope that he may succeed in winning the prize. Should this treatise, despite its imperfections, be so fortunate as to gain the prize, the author is confident that he will be able to expand it and improve it so as to justify the decision of the Academy.

1. [One of the copyists was List's daughter Emilie. The identity of the other copyist is not known.]

INDEX